MARRIED TO THE BRAND

Why Consumers Bond With Some Brands for Life

**LESSONS FROM 60 YEARS OF RESEARCH INTO
THE PSYCHOLOGY OF CONSUMER RELATIONSHIPS**

By William J. McEwen

GALLUP PRESS

Gallup Press
1251 Avenue of the Americas
23rd Floor
New York, NY 10020

First edition 2005

10 9 8 7 6 5 4 3 2 1

Library of Congress Control Number: 2005924915

ISBN: 1-59562-005-2

To Florence. My heart, my light, and my passion.

Married to the Brand

CONTENTS

Married to the Brand

≡ INTRODUCTION ≡

Marty has an important relationship — but it isn't just with his older brother, who lives in the same neighborhood. It's with Starbucks.

Every afternoon, Monday through Friday, Marty walks four and a half blocks to the Starbucks near his office. Sure, Marty can get coffee at work — his company provides it at no charge. Yet he leaves the office and walks past two other coffee shops to get to Starbucks, where he gladly pays $1.60 for something he could get for free just a few short steps from his desk. He does this even when it's raining.

It must be the coffee.

Truth be told, Marty probably couldn't taste the difference between his preferred Starbucks brew and whatever coffee is currently being poured by the folks at Diedrich or Peet's or Seattle's Best.

But when Marty walks into Starbucks, Jayson is already pouring him his grande Sumatra. Jayson calls out Marty's name and greets him with a welcoming smile. He leaves a bit of room in Marty's cup, because he knows Marty always adds half-and-half. Marty pays the $1.60, tosses his customary quarter in the tip jar, and climbs on a stool by the front window.

Marty isn't just buying coffee. He's buying an *experience*. He's buying a half-hour break from his desk — from his ringing phone and the relentless pings from his e-mail. This is an important interlude in Marty's day, and it costs him less than $2.

It's not that Starbucks coffee is "worth it." It's that Marty feels the Starbucks experience is worth it — and, even more importantly, that *he* is worth it. Starbucks is his personal moment in the day, and he would be hard-pressed to give up this ritual.

Now, it's important to note that Marty's relationship is not with a company, despite Starbucks' mission to be the "premier purveyor of the finest coffee in the world." Rather, it's a relationship grounded in the bond Marty feels for a particular Starbucks *store* — one of the more than 7,000 Starbucks locations now spread around the globe.

Marty gives something to Starbucks, Monday through Friday, but that's only because his favorite Starbucks store gives him something back. Lasting, meaningful relationships are always reciprocal.

But sometimes the return on Marty's investment doesn't quite match up to what he gets from his favorite Starbucks store. Two months ago, he was in another city, 3,000 miles from home. He arrived early for his 10 a.m. meeting and stopped by the Starbucks that was conveniently located in a hotel lobby just across the street. The Sumatra was the same, as were the logos, the napkins, and the familiar green background. But to Marty, it didn't feel much like *his* Starbucks. He joined the line of coffee seekers, then gave his order to the barista, who poured Marty's coffee, set it before him, and nodded with neither recognition nor enthusiasm. Marty sat at a small table, using his napkin to wipe away some spilled sugar. Somehow, it didn't feel quite right.

This may seem puzzling. Marty was clearly in a Starbucks store, similar to all the others. But there's a critically important difference between a Starbucks store and a Starbucks experience. To Marty and many thousands of customers just like him, the Starbucks experience is something more than the aprons, cups, beans, and décor. It's an experience that still varies from store to store, despite Starbucks' efforts to homogenize it. That's important, because if all Starbucks stores were like that big-city hotel lobby store, Marty's afternoon routine would probably be very different.

A Starbucks experience is all about the feeling Marty gets as a result of his visit. The taste may always be the same, and so may the cup. But the feeling can be different, because the experience can vary. Marty's feelings are the key to his Starbucks relationship — and the feelings of people like Marty are the key to Starbucks' future business success.

THE STORY OF THE CONSUMER

Much has been written about how Starbucks markets its products and about its expansion around the globe and into new categories and distribution channels. But these are stories about the Starbucks company.

This book doesn't tell the story of Starbucks or other companies. It's not about visionary entrepreneurs, marketing heads, or advertising agencies. Instead, it tells the story of consumers like Marty, because they determine the future success of any organization that markets branded products and services. This book is about how and why Marty — and millions of consumers like him — form relationships with brands.

There are real differences between what motivates a first purchase or visit and what turns that "first date" encounter into an ongoing relationship — a brand "marriage." Companies like Starbucks should never be satisfied with more first dates. Their financial success depends on their ability to build more marriages.

After all, Marty wasn't always a Starbucks customer. In fact, 15 years ago he had never heard of Starbucks. What brought Marty into Starbucks for the first time was curiosity. He wasn't looking to get married to Starbucks, and he wasn't even searching — at least consciously — for a new and different way to satisfy his desire for a daily break from the office. Then some of the folks at work started talking about a new place for coffee that had just opened up. One friend raved about the latte she had enjoyed the day before. Marty isn't a latte lover, but he was certainly interested in finding out for himself what the buzz was all about. So his first date with Starbucks took place, driven simply by Marty's curiosity about what he was hearing, and a feeling that maybe he'd like it.

But Marty's relationship with Starbucks didn't suddenly bloom when he sat and sipped his very first cup of coffee. Like all meaningful relationships, it evolved. It took shape over several months and through multiple "dating" experiences, as Marty determined, probably subconsciously, just where, how, and if Starbucks fit his life. His relationship evolved from a first encounter into what has become a true brand marriage: Starbucks is now an irreplaceable part of Marty's daily routine.

Now, Marty is not the sort of person who "marries" every brand with which he comes into regular contact. He doesn't have an emotional bond with his Vons grocery store, even though he buys his bottled water, salad dressing, and bananas there. He's not particularly committed to Sears, even though that's where he bought his blue sweater and his leaf blower. Yet he *does* have a relationship with Starbucks. What's the difference? Starbucks *connects* with Marty. Vons and Sears do not.

This book digs into what we now know about brand relationships, and what we've learned about the formation — and the value — of a genuine brand marriage. It looks at what it takes to keep a marriage healthy and explores what weakens, or even kills, a relationship.

RECIPROCAL RELATIONSHIPS

Not all brand marriages are between consumers and the stores where they shop or where they take their afternoon coffee breaks. Some brand relationships include a service component, where someone like Jayson interacts directly with the customers. But plenty of brand relationships involve a branded product and the consumer who buys or uses that product. These relationships range from beer to spark plugs to microwave ovens.

There are also situations in which businesses sell to other businesses, and in which relationships are formed between construction engineers and the companies that provide them with pre-stressed concrete, between IT managers and their software suppliers, or between physicians and pharmaceutical firms.

Brand marriages can be built and sustained in those situations, as well. But strong marriages aren't necessarily the norm, and marriage isn't the inevitable result of buying or using (or having "dated") a brand.

Marriage is more than a behavior.

SOMETHING SPECIAL

Consider a very different type of buying situation with a completely different consumer. When Eleanor pushes her cart down Aisle

6 at her neighborhood Ralphs supermarket and she needs salt, Eleanor always chooses Morton. Today, it costs 20 cents more than store-brand salt for the 26-ounce package. That's a price premium of just over 40%. Eleanor, like many seniors, is on a fixed income. Isn't the Ralphs brand salty enough?

Yet Eleanor spends her precious extra pennies on Morton Salt even though cheaper salt is available. She doesn't display the product to impress others. She buys Morton Salt because of the way it makes her feel. Like Marty, Eleanor doesn't feel the same way about all products, or about all brands. She's focused on only a few *special* brands — those that have won her heart as well as her mind. Bonds like these are what this book is all about.

Why is Eleanor so committed to Morton Salt? Her first date with the brand was fueled not by simple curiosity but by Eleanor's memories of her mom preparing her favorite lima bean casserole on Monday nights. Eleanor's marriage with Morton continues because no other brand of salt makes her feel just a little bit special — or evokes so many happy kitchen memories. That's why she'll pay those extra 20 cents.

Obviously, not all consumers feel like Eleanor. Some don't care about salt and are indifferent to whatever brands might be out there. Some are married not to Morton but to a store brand. In many product categories, store brands have about as many happy marriages as the "name" brands.

Regardless of the product or service category, not everyone who buys a brand marries it. Consumers who marry don't all marry the same brand. And they don't marry every brand they encounter.

HEARING THE VOICE OF THE CONSUMER

Eleanor and Marty are real people. They are only two consumers, but they represent many millions of others who have powerful stories to tell about the unique relationships they've formed with *some* of the brands they buy and use. This book gives voice to these consumers.

Marketing managers may have never heard Eleanor's or Marty's voice. That's because most of them focus on the overall statistics associated with large audiences of consumers. Customers, however, aren't simply statistics, and consumers aren't merely targets for marketing, passively awaiting cleverly crafted campaigns that will tell them what to buy — and when.

The Gallup Organization has been listening to consumers tell their stories for more than 60 years. We've talked with customers ordering lager in a British pub, and consumers buying cellular phones in Beijing. We've talked with shoppers strolling the malls and teens lined up at the fast-food window. We've also talked with mortgage brokers, physicians, and shipping company managers. We've heard about their brand experiences and about how brands — *some* brands — make them feel.

Our research shows that healthy brand marriages yield enormous financial value to a company and its stockholders. But this return will be realized only to the extent that these brands offer great value to the *consumer.*

Ultimately, *it is the consumer who controls the brand relationship.* It's not the MBA who may have been assigned as the "brand manager." Consumers decide whether they'll give their allegiance to brands like Morton Salt or Starbucks. Even when they do, this allegiance isn't offered for life. As with all too many marriages in this day and age, divorce is not uncommon, and "happily ever after" is largely the province of fairy tales.

TIES THAT BIND

Great brands such as Disney, Ritz-Carlton, Guinness beer, Nordstrom, and Singapore Airlines create exceptionally strong marriages with their customers. These companies have been written about elsewhere. Though these brands may have formed enduring bonds with their customers, it's important to remember that these are personal relationships that grow one customer at a time. And the thoughts and feelings of these companies' customers merit further exploration.

Married to the Brand draws an important new picture of the consumer. This book reveals the true nature of the emotional relationships consumers have with the brands they buy, the stores where they shop, the restaurants where they eat, and the banks to which they entrust their money.

This new picture of the consumer relationship is made possible by a unique approach to measuring and *managing* customer relationships, which have previously been considered important but impossible to measure — and thus, impossible to manage.

This book draws on new worldwide consumer research and development efforts completed between 2000 and 2004. It describes and defines the *emotional* attachment that is essential to bonding a consumer with a brand, to the point where no other brand will do. It is about the ultimate brand relationship: *passion* for the brand. And we're not just talking about passion for exciting luxury products such as BMW cars or Armani suits. We also mean passion for less "sexy" brands like Wal-Mart, FedEx, or Intel, or passion even for MasterCard, BP, or MCI.

We've studied world-class brand marriages and dug into what triggers the onset of a consumer connection — a first date. We've learned a great deal about the essential requirements for an *enduring* brand relationship: a lasting marriage between a company and a customer.

Married to the Brand shares this learning and discusses what it implies for managers and employees who are challenged to build strong brands and ensure lasting brand marriages. What we've learned applies not just in the boardroom, where brand strategies are typically formulated, but also to front-line employees who implement the strategies — who "live" the brand every day and either enhance or jeopardize it.

To take the first steps toward a brand relationship, listen to the voices of your customers. Their stories are often told in focus groups, but they're also told in large-scale quantitative surveys — if you ask the right questions.

CHAPTER ONE

A PATHWAY TO BRAND PASSION

For well over a half century, Gallup has been listening to consumers talk about brands — and about the special brands with which they've formed enduring emotional connections. And, in these millions of consumer interviews, we've also heard about initial relationships that turned sour.

What we've learned from digging into our consumer conversations will surprise some company managers, while reinforcing what others may have believed but haven't been able to prove. *Married to the Brand* is the result. The following conclusions summarize what we've learned and outline where we'll be heading in the chapters that follow:

+ Brand marriages aren't created overnight, regardless of how much money is spent on marketing programs or high-profile Super Bowl ads. True brand relationships aren't built in a day — even in the age of the Internet.

+ There's a crucial difference between a customer and an *engaged* customer. Gaining customers should never be a company's objective; building customer engagement should be.

+ Customer satisfaction programs haven't increased the numbers of healthy brand marriages; neither have most loyalty programs. This isn't because companies won't spend the money on these programs, or that they aren't serious about them. Rather, it's because programs like these have either missed or ignored what really drives the relationship. Besides, loyalty programs are readily duplicated by competitors, so they simply increase the cost of doing business while failing to address what it takes to make a brand marriage.

✦ What it takes to initially attract a first-time buyer or user is often quite different from what it takes to turn that prospect into a fully engaged customer. Dating is different from marriage. But both involve essential emotional connections that must be understood if they're ever going to be managed.

✦ Activating a new brand relationship (a first date) requires conveying a brand promise that is not just credible and compelling, but also establishes a personal connection with the potential customer. If the goal is an enduring brand marriage and not just a one-time fling, the brand has to begin building a platform for passion.

✦ Products alone can't support a passionate brand relationship, nor will low prices, great advertising, stunning packaging, or a superb location. They must all work together, since it is the total brand experience, and not just one isolated element, that determines the health of a brand marriage.

✦ Keeping customers (a brand marriage) involves adding meaningful depth to the bond that initially connects the consumer to the brand. Retaining customers goes beyond merely making a promise — it requires the performance of a total brand experience. For a healthy brand marriage, the company's brand promise must be kept on every subsequent date and at every brand touchpoint.

✦ In most cases, it's not enough that consumers trust a brand. That's because they may trust many brands — but somehow, the emotional connection goes no deeper than that. Trust is the essential foundation, and marriages won't last without it. For a lasting relationship, though, there must be brand passion.

✦ Most companies have strong brand relationships with only a small minority of their customers. Even great brands typically have healthy relationships with only about half of their customers — and they probably don't even know which ones they are.

✦ Companies in every industry have large numbers of customers with whom they have absolutely no relationship. Customer relationship management (CRM) programs and marketing promotions aren't shrinking the numbers of disaffected and disconnected customers. In many cases, they're actually creating more of them. They're not building brand marriages; they're creating climates for divorce.

✦ Emotions aren't merely warm and fuzzy concepts suitable mainly for greeting-card poetry and Hollywood scripts. Emotions are both powerful and profitable. Whether a company is marketing hamburgers or microprocessors, there's a demonstrable financial return that results from emotionally engaging customers — and there's a substantial cost that results from disengaging them.

✦ Every time a customer comes in contact with a company — with its products, stores, people, or ads, or with the stories that appear in the newspaper — the brand relationship can be enhanced. Or it can be diminished. Brand marriages aren't static; they continue to evolve.

✦ Brand relationship management isn't just a marketing challenge, nor is it a challenge that can be met solely through operational, product-development, or information technology enhancements. Successful marriage management can be achieved only by company-wide commitment and aligned, integrated efforts.

✦ Top-down corporate solutions to brand marriage management may offer great efficiencies — but they won't work. Relationship management begins not in the boardroom but at the individual customer interface.

Gallup's research has revealed that customer satisfaction isn't nearly enough to ensure an ongoing brand relationship. We've also learned that "loyalty" isn't enough and that "good" performance is woefully inadequate. That poses a huge problem. As Jim Collins has pointed out in his book *Good to Great*, too many companies become satisfied with "good" — and, he writes, "Good is the enemy of great." Marriages require more. Loving involves a whole lot more than liking.

PREACHING TO THE CHOIR?

Talking about brands and thinking about consumer relationships are hardly new. Bookstore shelves groan with books about brands, and legions of marketing managers spend sleepless nights wrestling with their brand challenges. CEO surveys by the Conference Board report that customer retention, organic growth, and brand loyalty remain high on the list of management concerns. In annual reports, companies announce that their aim is not merely to attract new customers, but to "satisfy" and "delight" them — or even to inspire customer "jubilation."

To meet these lofty goals, companies have challenged their marketing departments and enlisted the support of advertising agencies, public relations firms, and package designers. They've created customer relationship departments, supported by CRM software and led by customer relationship managers who are directly tasked with monitoring and managing the company's customer relationships.

How well is it working? To be blunt, it's not. Companies are wasting money and missing opportunities. Despite considerable expenditures, the evidence shows that most companies are *not* improving customer satisfaction or increasing customer loyalty. Most are *not* delighting their customers. Strong marriages remain the exception, rather than the rule.

The ACSI surveys conducted by the University of Michigan reveal that customer satisfaction index scores, regardless of industry, have not improved since the surveys began in 1994. In the overwhelming majority of cases, satisfaction trend lines are as flat as the proverbial pancake. One Gallup analysis found that only about 1 in 20 U.S. companies — a mere 5% — saw their customer scores improve in any consistent way over a 7–year period.

As a result, companies have become disappointed, disenchanted, and disillusioned. Bain's *Management Tools 2001* survey found that only one in four senior executives were "highly satisfied" with their efforts to measure and manage customer satisfaction. Perhaps that's why, as

Bain reported, the percentage of companies using some form of customer satisfaction measurement has sharply declined — from 86% in 1993 to only 60% in 2000.

Where are the jubilant customers? And what — or where — is the problem?

CHAPTER TWO

≡WHY CONSUMERS MARRY BRANDS≡

To understand the power of a strong brand relationship, it's helpful to begin with a short journey into the world of brands. Brands aren't just names that companies use to identify the various products and services they attempt to sell to people. Brands serve a greater purpose — not just for the marketer, but for the consumer, too.

Brands identify, define, and express the experience of using the particular products and services with which consumers connect. Brands are the partners in the dating dance, the entities with which individual consumers sometimes form important, reciprocal, and even loving relationships.

Brands are everywhere. They're inescapable: brands of autos, breakfast cereals, blue jeans, laser printers, law firms, discount brokerages, and grocery stores. They all cry out to be noticed, often simultaneously, seeking to entice consumers into a first date that each brand hopes will lead to a long-lasting, meaningful relationship.

Some of these brands succeed, but the vast majority do not. The brands that thrive offer a return to the customer, whether it's tangible or intangible, rational or emotional. And they provide this return each and every time the customer encounters the brand.

BRAND BUILDING AND BRAND BUZZ

As anyone interested in business management can attest, brands and brand management have been hot marketing (and book) topics in the business and academic worlds for at least the past 50 years. Having devoted all this time and brainpower to the subject, we should by now really understand what brands are, what it takes to entice a new customer, and what's required to keep that customer coming back time and again. You'd think we'd have already grasped the difference between passionate and indifferent consumers, and we'd know how to build strong brand marriages. Alas, we don't.

To be sure, we've all heard interesting anecdotes about the building of individual brands. Stories of brand champions and advertising architects abound: Herb Kelleher at Southwest Airlines, Helmut Panke at BMW, Ray Kroc at McDonald's ... the list goes on.

The business media are filled with compelling accounts of remarkable, but atypical, brand relationships. You've surely read about Harley-Davidson disciples, Linux lovers, and eBay groupies, and heard stories of brand "buzz," brand "cults," brand "tribes," and what the advertising leaders at Saatchi & Saatchi have dubbed consumer "Lovemarks." These stories are often provocative and intriguing. They describe passionate brand relationships that stimulate the sort of enthusiastic, even messianic, word-of-mouth brand proselytizing that some have called customer "evangelism."

But these brand stories seem to defy replication. There are precious few Harley-Davidsons, and today's hot brand may well be tomorrow's Pets.com, mired in Chapter 11. Trendy brands can turn out to be flash-in-the-pan, flavor-of-the-month fads.

What's more, these stories usually lack real *science* as to what makes a brand relationship great — and what keeps it that way. The evidence is anecdotal and conceptual, but there is precious little data to support the contentions and hypotheses that are posited as facts. In addition, these compelling accounts and books about brands offer little real guidance for company managers who operate in categories that don't generate much brand buzz, but who are nonetheless charged with creating energized brand relationships.

Brand building has been treated in two ways:

1. Some experts have viewed brand building in largely *formulaic* terms, grounding their arguments in the cold, hard world of

packaged-goods marketing. Unlike the anecdotal brand stories, they imply scientific rigor by laying out the steps to brand greatness in discrete, linear fashion. They posit deterministic, sequential decision frameworks with direct kinship to the old AIDA (Awareness, Interest, Desire, Action) model. And they may hold to their models despite the fact that they assume a linearity of "think-feel-do" that consumer data (such as that provided by the researchers at ad agency FCB) simply does not support. In addition, they imply management action that speaks more to the launch of Ivory soap or Vlasic Stackers than it does to the growth of Virgin, Nike, or iPod. They focus on the boardroom, without paying much attention to what happens at the store or the call center, where the proverbial rubber meets the customer road.

2. Other experts look upon brand development as primarily a *creative* process that results only from the dogged determination and unique insights of individual marketing visionaries like Akio Morita (Sony), Phil Knight (Nike), or Ernest Gallo (Gallo Wines). In this view, the brand development process is a "happy accident" that largely defies replication.

Though the old linear, deterministic models fall horribly short when it comes to accounting for human emotions, this does not mean brand building is a process that defies scientific inquiry. The formulaic approach falls short because it fails to include data relating to emotions. But that doesn't mean the creative approach is the right solution. Rigor and hard data can indeed contribute a great deal to what is still at its heart a creative brand-development process.

BRANDS AND BRAND DIFFERENTIATION: SENDING A MEANINGFUL MESSAGE

Brands have been in widespread use far longer than brand management has been discussed in marketing classrooms or company boardrooms. Brands were originally used by hunters and cattle herders as unique marks created to signify source or ownership. Their role was purely to *differentiate* one thing from another. The brand made a simple statement: "This one is mine; that one is yours."

With the rise of medieval guilds, these distinguishing ownership marks took on an additional role — one far more important to understanding brand relationships. As with artists' signatures, family crests, and heraldic emblems, distinguishing brand marks were used to communicate more than mere ownership. They were employed to convey important messages, some of which had to do with the status or position of the possessor. "Let no one doubt who I am." And some served as guarantors of product quality, conveying the particular pride felt by their creator or producer. "This is my work, and was made by none but me." "I stand behind this creation. You have my name on it."

The role of the brand was thus extended well beyond merely differentiating possessions: Brands now conveyed the personal endorsement of the product's creator as well as positive, enviable values associated with the ownership experience. They now expressed a *reciprocal relationship* — something that has value for both the owner and the maker.

BRAND DIFFERENTIATORS: ONLY PART OF THE SOLUTION

A great deal of work and expense typically goes into the development and design of brand differentiators. These range from distinctive logos to proprietary packages and unique product designs. But a marketer wants to create a great *brand*, not just ready recognition along a highway or on a supermarket shelf.

Consumers must be aware of a brand's existence before they can bond with it. But brand-name awareness is actually a very poor way to express the greatness of an established brand. It's a terrible measure of the strength of a brand relationship; in most cases, it's not even a very good indicator of the likelihood of a first date. PanAm was a familiar name, but that familiarity didn't halt the airline's demise. Ditto for Plymouth and MG automobiles. Oldsmobile is still a well-remembered name, but it's no longer a great brand. Enron is a very well-known name, but — well, you get the picture.

Let's be clear: If you're a marketer, *the goal isn't brand name awareness. The goal is a brand marriage.* The goal is a genuine, lasting connection between consumers and your brand.

Creating a differentiated brand name or look is the easy part. The real challenge is creating a unique brand experience — a distinct feeling that results from buying, using, or dating the brand. The brand experience, not the name or logo, is the basis for a brand relationship.

Brands die, not because they lack a unique look, but because they suffer a shortage of passionate consumer relationships. They die because they've stopped attracting new suitors, and they've let their existing customer marriages deteriorate. Quite simply, there are just not enough consumers who care.

Increasing the numbers of those who care is the marketing challenge. To meet that challenge, you must look at differentiation through the eyes of the consumer.

CUSTOMERS COUNT

It's up to consumers to determine whether alternative brands are different enough when it comes to the factors that matter. Some consumers see vast differences between Pepsi and Coke or think flying JetBlue is a totally different airline experience. Others don't.

There are people around the world who are a lot like Tom, a manager with a business services firm on the U.S. West Coast. Tom owns a car, and when he travels, he often rents one, up to 20 times a year. But ask him about autos, and he'll tell you they're all about the same. He feels no difference, whether he's behind the wheel of his own three-year-old Buick or sitting in a rented Taurus, Galant, or Monte Carlo.

Tom's good friend Walter, on the other hand, is a car buff who can't understand Tom's comment that "A car is a car. They're all the same to me." To Walter, every car is different and some autos, like his cherished Morgan, are truly special.

Walter sees vast and important differences between auto brands, whether it's in their styling, dashboard instrumentation, or interior design. He says he can *feel* the differences in engine performance and gear ratios. But to Tom, these differences are trivial. A car is just a means for him to get from point A to point B, and no amount of Super Bowl commercials or enthusiastic *Car & Driver* product reviews will convince him otherwise.

What accounts for the difference between Tom and Walter? For a marketer, the challenge is to identify the differences between the Toms and the Walters, so the company can focus its efforts on talking to each kind of customer in a way that recognizes the differences between them.

A SEA OF SAMENESS

Our research shows that whether we're talking about beer, banking, or business services, there are actually a great many Toms, and there are also a great many Walters. And there are some essential ingredients in the making — and in the care and feeding — of a customer like Walter.

In one recent survey, almost one-quarter (24%) of U.S. car owners stated that, in their eyes, there are no real differences between the various auto brands. They agree with Tom. Yet almost one in five (19%) auto owners feel there is only one car for them: a car they believe stands out as different from — and better than — all the rest.

Standing out is certainly not easy, given the sheer numbers of options available. If you're interested in a midsize sedan, Edmunds.com lists more than 40 different ones, ranging alphabetically from the Acura RL to the Volvo S80, and that's just considering the 2005 model year. If you want to consider the popular sport utility vehicle, expect to add 40-plus possibilities to your list. Checking *Consumer Reports* can help, because it doesn't road-test every vehicle. And even this assistance will only narrow your list of midsize family vehicles to about 20.

Given the confusing array of overlapping and similar-looking vehicles, it's understandable that a quarter of U.S. auto owners see little difference between the available makes and models.

A check of other product and service categories reveals comparable results. Regardless of the actual number of aggressively competing brands, U.S. consumers see only a sea of sameness:

+ Over half (58%) of U.S. banking customers state that they see no differences between banks.

+ Almost half of past-year domestic U.S. fliers (45%) feel that all airlines are "the same."

+ Over half (54%) of online product purchasers say that all Web site marketers are the same.

This does *not* mean that consumers can't tell a Volkswagen Beetle from a BMW Z4. Instead, it says that consumers believe they're surrounded by a bevy of brands that look and *feel* the same, in part because there's a cacophony of brand communications that trumpet essentially the same promises. Looking through the consumers' lenses, the alleged differences in car model styling — or in bank checking account fees and ATM locations — simply *don't matter*.

Where there are no meaningful differences, brands become interchangeable commodities, differentiated only by what's cheapest or easiest to access.

BUILDING MEANINGFUL DIFFERENTIATION: ATTRIBUTES VERSUS BENEFITS

In the search for meaningful brand differentiation, companies and brand managers must bear in mind that brand *attributes* are not the same as brand *benefits*. This seems obvious, yet companies constantly confuse the two.

Attributes represent the features, aspects, ingredients, or components of a product that can be objectively verified. They are services the company provides or the ingredients it puts in its products: Examples are a gel toothpaste with stannous fluoride added, a fiber optic connection, or a sport utility vehicle with leather seats, on-demand four-wheel drive, and a moonroof.

These characteristics may be unique to a single brand: For instance, only Budweiser beer is "beechwood aged," and only Castrol GTX motor oil has "unique polarized molecules." Characteristics (such as leather seats) may also be shared by many competing brands. Either way, they represent brand features that are discernible, essentially verifiable, and sometimes even legally protected.

However, these features may or may not represent benefits to the buyer and user. *Benefits*, in contrast, represent the features or characteristics that consumers feel are directly and discernibly related to the performance and attractiveness of the product or the product-use experience.

Benefits are what the consumer values, rather than what the company advertises. These are the returns that merit a consumer's investment as a brand buyer, user, and potential marriage partner. Benefits exist solely in the eye of the beholder and represent what the consumer takes away from the brand experience, based on whatever needs — real or perceived, rational or emotional — he or she might have.

Most companies live in a world of brand attributes, because they have to manufacture the products, set up the store operations, and design the packages, processes, and policies that are essential to whatever they're marketing. Companies focus on what they make and how they make, package, and deliver it.

But consumers don't live in the world of attributes; benefits are what matter most to them. They answer the question "What's in it for *me*?" Benefits build marriages.

BRAND BENEFITS AND BRAND PASSION

Ask Diane about her favorite grocery store, and she'll tell you what she thinks are its unique benefits. But ask her to comment on a lengthy list of its features, ranging from the number of checkout counters to its ready-to-eat meals and "buy one, get one free" program, and she responds:

> "Mainly, I like the atmosphere. A lot of the employees say, 'Hi.' They're really friendly, and that means a lot to me."

Diane doesn't mention the number of spaces in the parking lot, the wide selection of yogurt flavors, the five different kinds of lettuce, or the low prices for this week's featured specials. These features may support her choice, but they're not what make her passionate about the store. What Diane values is its atmosphere, which represents a unique and important store benefit — something she feels her store has, and other stores don't.

This same focus on brand benefits is evident when consumers talk about the products they buy, not just the stores where they buy them. Listen to how Heather states her case for Neutrogena:

> "Neutrogena is the perfect product for me. I've always had severe, severe skin problems. And Neutrogena changed my life, basically. I know that sounds a little silly, but it has. It's cleared up my skin and made me a confident person. I can't live without it."

Heather doesn't mention that Neutrogena is dermatologist-tested, that it's uniquely transparent, or that it's now available in a pump bottle. Though endorsement by dermatologists may reassure her and provide rational support for her choice, what Heather focuses on are the end-benefits she receives: clear skin and a confident outlook. Those are the reasons why Heather "can't live without" Neutrogena.

TABLE STAKES: THE SEARCH FOR UNIQUE BENEFITS

It sounds so simple: To start a dating relationship that might lead to a brand marriage, companies must communicate their products' benefits. But it's not that easy. That's because the most highly valued and sought-after product and service benefits can almost never be claimed by a single brand.

Though only one brand of photographic film may lay claim to distinctive yellow packaging, many others will claim to offer "sharp, true-to-life color." Only one beer brand may be "beechwood aged," but many brands claim to deliver "real beer taste." Many PC makers boast of "reliable performance."

Thus, all marketers face a Catch-22 dilemma: *Attributes with little apparent value or meaning to consumers are readily associated with a single brand, while attributes that connote real benefits get copied by the competition.* So, paradoxically, whatever is most important is often least likely to be a differentiator between brands.

This is true in every category where brands and companies compete. Any number of vehicles feature leather seats and moonroofs, and most manufacturers offer models that feature four-wheel drive. Many luxury-car dealers now offer a free car wash and a loaner car to their service customers. Any number of banks offer 5-minute teller access, convenient ATMs, and free checking. None of these features is a brand differentiator.

Valued attributes and important end-benefits become what we call "table stakes": They represent the price of entry that's required not to win, but merely to compete. To get a seat at the table, all beers must promise "real beer taste," all PCs must promise "reliable performance," and all hotels must promise a "clean and comfortable room."

Consumers not only expect these table-stakes benefits, they demand them. But these are simply parity promises that portend parity brand experiences. They don't provide the basis for a lasting brand marriage.

There *are* some great brands that have successfully created benefit-based brand differentiation, often supported by tangible product attributes. They have built enduring emotional connections — but they have done so slowly, and over time.

When Charles talks about his favorite brand of photographic film, he begins by relating some basic, table-stakes benefits that, while important, can also be claimed by other brands. But he concludes by expressing the unique emotional connection that he feels. This emotional bond, unlike a product feature, is something that cannot be readily usurped by a competitor:

> "I've used a lot of different kinds of film. I sometimes use the bargain brand. But Kodak is dependable. The color is great. The brilliancy of the print is great, and you always will have a product that will have lasting memories."

Other brands may promise "great" color or "brilliant" prints. But as far as Charles is concerned, only one brand delivers "lasting memories." That's what brand passion is all about — creating a powerful *emotional* bond with a brand.

CHAPTER THREE

BRAND RELATIONSHIPS: WHY COMPANIES SHOULD CARE

Take a stroll through any supermarket. In stores around the globe, you'll typically find the dating dance floor extremely crowded with brands struggling to be noticed and chosen for a first date. In the United States, the average supermarket stocks 35,000 to 40,000 branded items, but only a few will find a place in the wobbly-wheeled carts of hurried grocery shoppers. Small wonder, then, that so many brands wither and die.

The graphic "The Route to a Great Brand Relationship" shows how a brand marriage evolves. The bonds are first formed through an initial encounter — the first date that signals the start of a potentially reciprocal relationship. Only after the brand courtship ritual, which may actually consist of many dates, does a brand marriage begin to take form.

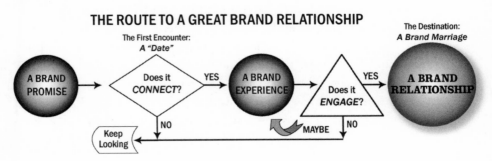

THE ROUTE TO A GREAT BRAND RELATIONSHIP

The final marriage destination has a distinctive sound and feel. Its nature is revealed by listening to consumers talk about their experiences and their feelings as customers.

We've talked with thousands of happily married, highly engaged consumers — shoppers like Pamela, who proudly proclaims her feelings about Miracle Whip:

> "If they were to stop making Miracle Whip, my life would end. I have been known to get up and make a sandwich in the middle of the night. If there's no Miracle Whip, I will wake my husband up to go buy me a jar. I am passionate about my club sandwiches, and I am passionate about Miracle Whip."

We've also talked with a great many shoppers who are *not* like Pamela. They're more like Helene, who, when asked about the white wine she was buying, said:

> "I really don't care. I basically buy whatever is cheapest. I hate to admit it, but I can't tell the difference between any of these. I just mix it with cranberry juice, and it all tastes pretty much the same."

But what difference does it make what people say about the brands they buy or how they feel? After all, isn't it what they actually *do* that counts?

MONEY MATTERS: THE PAYOFF

Actually, for a company interested in managing its customer relationships, how customers feel — and how they have come to feel that way — matters a great deal. It matters because Pamela will pay more for her Miracle Whip than she would for an essentially identical salad dressing product. She'll shell out more cash, or she'll go without.

Helene, because of her lack of a brand relationship (at least when it comes to white wine), behaves quite differently from Pamela: She will not pay more for a particular brand of wine. A product with a more attractive label or a more familiar name — even an award-winning, better brand — isn't worth the extra money to her.

A Pamela-type of brand relationship is, to any marketer, delightfully different from a Helene-type of relationship. Most recently, Pamela paid $1.36 more for Miracle Whip than she would have for a jar of Vons grocery-store-brand salad dressing. For Kraft, this is a price premium of 50% beyond what they (and Vons) could otherwise command based simply on the value of the ingredients.

That's only because, as Pamela views it, she isn't buying salad dressing to spread on her sandwich. She's buying Miracle Whip, which she feels is the perfect — and only acceptable — complement to her special club sandwich. She feels it tastes a little tangier and spreads more easily. Pamela has used Miracle Whip for years and trusts the contents of every jar to be exactly the same. So what she's really purchasing is peace of mind and the reassurance of knowing her club sandwich will always be perfect. It seems a fair return for her $1.36 investment.

It's important to remember, however, that the world does not consist of "fully engaged" customers who have a passionate connection with every brand they encounter, and "disengaged" customers who have no emotional bond to any of the brands in their pantries.

Pamela and Helene are not types. Their brand engagement or disengagement varies by category. Pamela may be engaged to her brand of salad dressing, but disengaged from her bank, her grocery store, or her mobile phone provider.

Pamela cares deeply about Miracle Whip but not about the brand of bacon she uses in her sandwich. Helene doesn't care about which white wine she loads into her shopping cart. Yet she flies only on American Airlines and buys her meats only at Stew Leonard's grocery — and she will loudly and proudly tell people why.

How can a company turn some of its indifferent relationships into passionate ones? How can it avoid having its best advocates — those who are married to the brand, as Pamela is with Miracle Whip — slip away until they become apathetic, much like Helene is with white wine? To answer those questions, we must deepen our understanding of the destination — toward a fully engaged brand marriage — and the factors that enhance or jeopardize that type of bond.

INVESTING IN BRAND RELATIONSHIPS

Creating or protecting strong brand relationships isn't easy, but it's worth the effort. No brand will ever marry 100% of its customers, but every brand should strive to create more marriages. We've seen companies where 30%, 40%, 50%, or even 60% of their customers are like

Pamela — and we've seen other companies where there are almost no Pamelas.

Let's assume that there are 10 million Pamelas putting quart jars of Miracle Whip into their shopping carts four times a year. That's $54 million more in revenue than what Kraft — and Vons, because the grocer shares in these profits — would have received for sales of a plain-label "salad dressing." It's $54 million each year Kraft and Vons wouldn't receive if they had no passionate Pamelas.

In their efforts to create more Pamelas, businesses have invested millions of dollars in establishing and supporting the brands they market. In 2004, companies (including Kraft) invested somewhere in the neighborhood of $166 billion in the United States alone to advertise their brands. Yet advertising is only one part — though a large portion, to be sure — of a company's total marketing expense. In addition to advertising expense, companies shell out for consumer promotions, incentives to retailers, event sponsorships, product enhancements, public relations campaigns, label redesigns, and a host of other ongoing brand marketing activities.

This all adds up to a lot of money. If we consider just the advertising expenditures for 2004, companies spent an average of more than $570 for each woman, man, and child in the United States — and they're likely to continue to spend this amount or more each year.

Companies could spend this money in any number of other ways. They could build more manufacturing plants or purchase more product ingredients, labels, and jars. They could just put the money in their corporate pockets or return it to their shareholders. But they don't. They spend the money on brand marketing — even if, as we've learned, they don't necessarily invest it wisely. Companies do this because they firmly believe their brands represent important investments that will pay continuing dividends not just in the next quarter or two, but year after year.

BRAND MARRIAGES ARE COMPANY ASSETS

Companies create brands and support them because brands represent company assets that can be leveraged, bought, and sold. When assessing the worth of a company, analysts and investors assign an important price premium to the intangible goods associated with a brand name.

The difference between the value of the company's identifiable, tangible assets and its total assessed worth to investors is a measure of the brand equity associated with the brands the company has built and nurtured over the years. The Coca-Cola Company, for example, is worth far more than the value of its trucks, offices, warehouses, and bottling or syrup-making facilities. In 2004, Interbrand estimated that the Coca-Cola brand was worth more than $67 billion.

Ultimately, neither the size of the company nor its total annual business volume determines the value of its brand name. According to the same Interbrand research, the Mercedes brand is worth about 50% more than the Ford brand. Similarly, the Chanel brand is more valuable than Kraft, and the Tiffany brand is worth more than Boeing.

THE MOST VALUABLE GLOBAL BRANDS 2004

BusinessWeek/Interbrand ranking of the world's top brands

Rank	Brand	Brand Value $USD Millions
1	Coca-Cola	67,394
2	Microsoft	61,372
3	IBM	53,791
4	GE	44,111
5	Intel	33,499
6	Disney	27,113
7	McDonald's	25,001
8	Nokia	24,041
9	Toyota	22,673
10	Marlboro	22,128
11	Mercedes	21,331
12	Hewlett-Packard	20,978
13	Citibank	19,971
14	American Express	17,683
15	Gillette	16,723
16	Cisco	15,948
17	BMW	15,886
18	Honda	14,874
19	Ford	14,475

Rank	Brand	Brand Value $USD Millions
20	Sony	12,759
21	Samsung	12,553
22	Pepsi	12,066
23	Nescafé	11,892
24	Budweiser	11,846
25	Dell	11,500

Source: *BusinessWeek*, August 2, 2004, pp. 68-69

It's hardly surprising, then, that companies see investing in brands as smart business. These brand investments yield high returns — $1.36 at a time, thanks to Pamela, or many millions of dollars at a time, thanks to the analysts and investors who count on customers like Pamela to continue spending their money supporting the brands they love.

Thus, brands warrant a company's investment. However, there is no payback from these investments unless *consumers* get a return on *their* investment.

CHAPTER FOUR

BRAND ENCOUNTERS:
CONNECTING WITH CONSUMERS

To stay healthy, companies must be able to attract new customers as well as sustain and grow their relationships with existing ones. Old customers die off or may, as a result of changes in life stage, outgrow their need for particular products or brands. Thus, every brand must continue to attract first dates and entice fresh new prospects into the fold.

Those first, tentative dates must turn into second dates, and third dates — and eventually, if all goes according to plan, into healthy brand marriages. *True brand greatness is reflected in the number of strong brand marriages, not just in the number of prospects who are aware of the brand or who may have been enticed into a single first-date experience.*

Consumers don't start out as fully engaged, committed customers. Pamela wasn't born with a passion for Miracle Whip, nor was Marty innately drawn to Starbucks. And Tom isn't genetically indifferent to all auto brands. These relationships and non–relationships evolved.

Each brand relationship begins with an initial transaction that represents the customer's first direct personal experience with the brand. That initial experience is itself an outcome, however, because it's usually the end result of a number of pre-purchase encounters between the consumer and the brand.

These courtship encounters are often both brief and casual. They range from seeing the brand — the potential date — in the marketplace (for example, on a shelf, on the road, in the mall, or in an office building) to reading or hearing about it (through television ads, Web sites, and brochures, as well as in articles and reviews). Encounters also may include contact with various brand representatives, such as company employees or salespeople.

Importantly, pre-purchase brand encounters often include contact with people who are (or were) brand buyers or users — people who may be happily married to the brand or, perhaps, bitterly divorced. Encounters like these are enormously powerful in determining which brands get chosen and which ones remain on the sidelines.

Sometimes these initial brand encounters all seem to convey one clear brand message, such as Harley-Davidson's promise of raw, macho power or Tiffany's allure of sophisticated elegance. But in many cases, these encounters convey messages that are unfocused or even contradictory — messages too muddled to inspire a first date.

Managing these pre-purchase brand encounters is a formidable task. Bear in mind that a company controls only some of these encounter-based brand messages, such as advertising campaigns, package designs, store layouts, and press releases. But it doesn't dictate word-of-mouth from other customers, stories on "60 Minutes," or buzz on the Internet. And it doesn't determine what the competition does or what it offers.

Recognizing the multiplicity of brand-relevant messages — and that the impact of traditional advertising campaigns may pale in comparison to that of Web sites and blogs — companies are actively exploring new ways to meet consumers. These include everything from product placement in movies to interactive Web sites that allow consumers to play games and take a more active role in determining the messages they receive from companies.

Regardless of whether these initial encounters are consistent in what they say about a brand, each one conveys an expectation of brand performance — or non-performance.

IN THE BEGINNING:
CREATING CONNECTIONS AND OVERCOMING THE HURDLES

The path to an ongoing brand relationship begins with the brand promise. But reception and awareness of that promise are merely the first step. Consumers are aware of many brands that they don't or won't buy.

There's a more critical prerequisite: Does the brand promise *connect* with consumers? Prospects must look on the promised experience as something that's not only unique and desirable but that also speaks directly and personally to them. Prospects must be able to readily envision themselves as brand users or customers — and they should have some feeling for what that might mean to them personally.

Unless the company's brand promise establishes an emotional connection between the prospect and the brand, any subsequent experience through a promotion — such as free trials or coupons — won't create a lasting bond. Coupons and discounts may prompt a first date, but on their own, they aren't a sufficient basis for an enduring marriage. Coupons are essentially bribes; they create bonds that last only until the next bribe is offered. When the company stops the discount — when an auto manufacturer discontinues its 0% financing offer, for example — the customer relationships may also disappear.

Even when the brand promise connects, however, there may be barriers and speed bumps on the road to a brand relationship.

Some conditions make moving to a new relationship more complicated. This is particularly true when switching brands is difficult or even impossible. For example, if contractual relationships tie consumers to their current brand or provider, switching may be enormously complicated. In situations like these, companies can use incentives and promotions to overcome the potential costs of or difficulties in switching, and to move prospects along the road to a strong marriage.

If switching difficulties can be overcome, then a brand promise that connects will result in a first date. At that point, firsthand experience becomes critically important. Second dates depend on what happens during the first ones.

But it all starts with the brand promise.

PROMISES WITH POTENTIAL

Not all brand promises are created equal; they're not all equally capable of triggering a passionate relationship. The ones that have this potential can vary quite widely in their content. But when the goal is a first date that creates the foundation for a brand relationship, a solid brand promise produces a positive consumer response to each of the following questions:

+ Is it credible?

+ Is it compelling?

+ Does it connect with the prospective partner?

The graphic "Turning a Prospect Into a Customer" highlights the first portion of the brand relationship path. It illustrates the process from an initial pre-purchase brand encounter to a first date. It shows the hurdles that must be overcome to activate an initial trial relationship and encourage consumers to test the brand's potential for a meaningful and enduring relationship.

TURNING A PROSPECT INTO A CUSTOMER

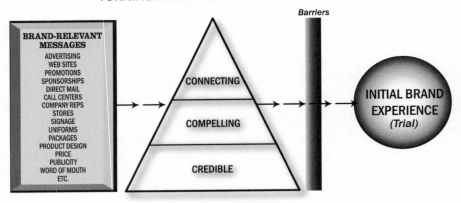

PROMISES THAT CONNECT

There's no easy solution to the challenge of identifying a brand promise powerful enough to attract new customers. No one hot-button exists, nor is there a singles-bar "What's your sign?" come-on line that's a slam dunk. The first date is up to consumers.

If the goal is a brand marriage, then we must dismiss courtship promises that may generate a first date but not a lasting relationship. Promises that can't be kept, or won't be kept long-term, will prove ineffective. Declarations like "Miracle cure," "Free!" "Lose 20 pounds in 20 minutes," or "Will grow hair on a billiard ball" are no more likely to build marriages than "Hey, sailor. In town long?"

However, there *are* certain types of promises that have shown — when their timing is right — that they can emotionally connect with prospects. They set a foundation for more than a one-time fling. But their potential is realized only when these brand promises are credibly presented and compellingly supported. These include:

✦ **Problem/Solution**. One of the oldest and unfortunately most abused techniques for connecting with consumers is the problem/solution approach. Here, the brand promises to provide a unique solution to a consumer's concerns. This approach fails when companies focus on trivial problems or solutions that lack credibility. This has frequently been the case in so-called slice-of-life advertising, where stereotypical housewives try to convince their neighbors that the latest washday marvel will magically heal spousal rifts and make life once again worthwhile.

When the identified problems are both real and personally relevant and the solutions are clear and direct, however, this approach can build an immediate connection with prospects. That's because when the problem/solution approach is honest and well-executed, it creates a feeling of recognition: "Hey — that's *me!*" That's the basis for a powerful personal connection.

Burger King once used this approach, telling fast-food customers that they didn't have to settle for a one-type-fits-all burger; instead, at Burger King, you could "Have it your way." OnStar vehicle navigation systems have vividly demonstrated the benefits of their service as a solution to problems ranging from inadvertent lockouts to stolen cars. FedEx has dramatized the problems of missed overnight deliveries and combined that with a reassuring promise that packages will "absolutely, positively" reach their destinations on time.

✦ **Reassurance**. In situations where brand performance has been notoriously uneven and consumers feel they have been burned, a brand can generate the potential for passion by offering vital — and total — peace-of-mind reassurance to the prospective buyer. This can be a powerful motivator.

A study conducted for a new telecommunications service provider revealed that none of the company's brand promises was capable of interesting prospects in a first date, even though many of the company's attributes were verifiably superior to the competition's. Prospects were unimpressed by its wide variety of available cutting-edge products, its unmatched international capabilities, or its impressive technological resources and expertise. They were even unmoved by the company's offering of a lower price.

What *did* intrigue prospects was an absolute reassurance of freedom from problems. The reason was simple: In the country in which the company was introducing its services, customers had been regularly, sometimes spectacularly, disappointed by service interruptions, communications breakdowns, and unacceptable signal quality. They weren't interested in cheaper — only in better. And in this case, "better" was defined as peace-of-mind reliability rather than cutting-edge technological wizardry.

As with problem/solution promises, a performance reassurance promise must be credible to be motivating — which is why reassurance promises resonate most profoundly when they are delivered by objective third parties such as *Consumer Reports* or through a friend's or a reviewer's testimonial. FedEx succeeded in delivering a reassurance promise that was both unique and meaningful in a world in which broken promises and missed deliveries had become the norm.

A brand can also create a connection by serving consumers as a "badge," or an outward sign that tells the world something about the buyer or user. Several have been used regularly, with varying degrees of success:

✦ **Prestige**. The brand badge may be one of status, indicating that the customer is someone special, someone apart from the ordinary. Many brands — Montblanc pens, Louis Vuitton purses, Jaguar cars, and Rolex watches, to name a few — seek to signal prestige. But consumers won't necessarily think a brand is elegant just because it comes with a high price tag. We've found similarly priced luxury autos that differ greatly, in terms of the pride consumers associate with having one in their garage. We've also observed expensive, upscale retail stores that generate far less pride among their shoppers than do the low-priced retailers with whom they sometimes compete. Price does *not* equal prestige.

+ **Personal qualities**. Other badge promises attempt to convey the personal qualities associated with a brand's buyer or owner. The range of these personal characteristics is extremely broad and can be seen in many product and service categories. The "young and alive" badge of the Pepsi generation was used to characterize "those who think young." Merrill Lynch's "bullish" advertising was designed to appeal to individual investors who saw themselves as "smart" and "savvy." Nike invests its shoe wearers with a badge of "competitive determination" and a "never give up" quality.

Badge messages — whether they focus on promises of prestige or other personal qualities — can vary widely. But they will connect only to the extent that their personal characteristics are highly desirable and the brand association is credible.

+ **Membership**. A brand may even come to represent a membership card, conveying a special oneness with others who share a dating or marriage relationship with the same brand. Many Harley-Davidson owners, Linux users, Porsche drivers, Manchester United fans, and JetBlue fliers feel this way. Thus, a first date with a brand may commence because of the seeming attractiveness of the potential brand fraternity.

+ **Memory triggers**. Brands can also serve as powerful personal reminders, established through strong and direct associations with special moments or memories. To Eleanor, Morton Salt in her cupboard harkens back to a time of family meals, warm kitchens, and tableside conversations.

A conversation with Shari also illustrates this important brand function:

> "My family always used Ragú spaghetti sauce when I was young. After college, I started making my own. Once in a while, if I'm in the mood for comfort food, I'll make up a batch of Ragú spaghetti and it just makes me feel better."

In cases such as these, the first date is, in essence, a blind date, arranged by parents or friends who may be long gone but whose memory lingers pleasantly. Not all brands can successfully conjure up these memories or leverage the associated feelings; not all consumers necessarily value what Mom or Dad or Grandma once did. For brands that do, however, memory can be a powerful incentive for a first date.

✦ **Self-completion**. Finally, brands may serve consumers as a means of self-completion, adding significant emotional values that help customers bridge the gap between the person they feel they are and the person they might aspire to be. Marlboro capitalized on smokers' desires to see themselves as rugged, individualistic cowboys, not simply as people who huddle outside office buildings in the cold or rain to get their nicotine fix.

Self-completion promises often serve as an endorsement of the customer's self-worth, simply because, as L'Oreal ads have said, "I'm worth it." In these cases, the first date occurs as a result of an emotional trigger, such as a perception of a perfect fit between the consumer and what the brand represents. Here, the promise focuses not on what *is* but on what the consumer wishes it might be.

This aspect of the brand relationship is similar to what Douglas Holt has labeled "identity brands." These brands are qualitatively different from the badge brands mentioned above. Brands that self-complete reflect not just status or prestige but a particular personal identity the consumer dreams about or longs for. These brand messages are as much a personal, internal statement to customers as they are an external message to their friends and neighbors.

BROKEN PROMISES AND MISSED OPPORTUNITIES

When brand promises are made, far too often they're of a "me too" variety and spark no pangs of potential passion in consumers. Even generic table-stakes promises are often broken. Customers are enticed or bribed into a first date — a visit, a single transaction, or a short-term relationship. But when the relationship is weakened through inattention, ineptitude, or inconsistent promise delivery, consumers immediately or eventually sever it. But it doesn't have to be that way.

CHAPTER FIVE

BEGINNING A
LASTING RELATIONSHIP

Consider a hotel where you've stayed recently. It may have made its brand promise to you through advertising, promotions, brochures, a Web site, its reservations clerks, or a combination of these. That promise may have been reinforced by travel-magazine articles or reviews that you've read.

Keeping that brand promise, however, involves a much greater range of contact, including your impressions of the hotel's external appearance, the desk clerk's efficiency, and your room's condition and furnishings. It may have included the appetite appeal of the room-service salad, the speed of the business center's computers, or even the availability of towels by the pool.

Keeping the brand promise involves aspects that the hotel's management can control, including its location, the room size, and pricing; aspects it indirectly controls, such as the warmth and efficiency of the hotel staff; and also those over which it has little or no control, like the inadvertent fire alarm, and the next-door-neighbor who decides to bellow off-key arias at 2 a.m.

Now, multiply your single hotel experience by the duration in days of the average hotel stay. Then multiply that by as many as 499 different properties, and that suggests only part of the challenge confronting companies like Hilton Hotels. Each Hilton property has myriad opportunities to keep or default on its brand promise. Each room, restaurant, housekeeper, telephone operator, or maintenance worker can make a difference. Every point of contact is challenged to deliver the same brand promise with the same degree of professionalism, polish, and performance — every time. Consistent performance at every customer touchpoint is essential if the brand promise is to be more than an empty and toothless slogan.

CONNECTING ... AND FAILING TO CONNECT

Most initial brand encounters don't turn into dates, most dates don't turn into marriages, and most brand marriages don't last. Divorces are even more common in the brand world than they ever were in Reno.

For decades, as many as 80% of new grocery-store offerings have failed to last a season. Some reports put the current new-product failure rate at a whopping 94%. Yet they were all created by teams of hardworking product-development experts. Most were tested, and lots of data were collected from target consumers. These products were introduced into the marketplace with intriguing brand names, distinctive logos, and attractive packaging. They were placed prominently on grocery store shelves, though many grocers now charge for this privilege through slotting allowances. And they were advertised, often with heavy television support, and backed by campaigns crafted by award-winning copywriters and guided by strategic planners.

And they failed.

They failed, and they continue to fail, because they're heading in the wrong direction. They don't concentrate on building brand relationships. They focus instead on registering a brand name with consumers, creating awareness of its advertising, producing attractive packaging, and developing intriguing promises. They focus on what it takes to create a first date, but *not* on what it takes to turn that date into a lasting marriage. They create unique brand names and parity brand experiences. In short, there's nothing to connect *with*.

This is a problem across all industries. Once-proud leaders in the automotive world, Plymouth and Oldsmobile are no more (or very soon will be); they've gone the way of the Studebaker, the Edsel, the Packard, and the DeSoto. Airlines merge, department stores merge, banks and brokerages acquire or get absorbed, and familiar brand names disappear. Web site and dot-com marketers move overnight from the penthouse to the bankruptcy courts.

"I AM THE GREATEST"

Let's return to the beginning. If a brand is, at its very essence, a promise made by a company, then the promise must be meaningful. It must also be communicated and shared internally with the company's "promise keepers" and externally with its customers and prospects.

There are three requirements for a brand promise: it must be credible, compelling, and able to personally connect with consumers. Each of these three requirements is worth exploring in a bit of depth, because the brand promise is what sets the stage for any ensuing brand relationship.

First, the promise must not only be heard by prospective buyers, triers, or daters, it must be believed. The promise must have *Credibility*.

This does not mean, however, that consumers must immediately and completely embrace each new promise. Potentially powerful promises may well produce an initially skeptical response ("I wonder if they could actually do that"). There's an important difference, as researchers at the Leo Burnett ad agency demonstrated decades ago, between generating curiosity (the desire to learn more) and provoking outright disbelief — a total rejection of the company's intended message. Promises that pique curiosity can stimulate consumers to dig deeper, search further, and test an intriguing proposal. Curiosity about the brand promise may prompt a date. Rejection of that promise will not.

Overcoming this first Credibility hurdle may seem simple, but it's actually quite a challenge. Some marketing consultants contend that mass-media advertising, the vehicle traditionally used to share the brand promise, has lost its impact. Others claim advertising is dead, either because it has strayed from its core challenge (which should be selling, not entertaining) or because years of overstated and unkept promises have hardened the consumer audience to even the most creative advertising appeals. According to these pundits, publicity and word-of-mouth buzz are what now build brands, simply because these are the message vehicles that have Credibility with consumers.

PLEASE BELIEVE ME ...

Our research into categories ranging from autos to frozen dinners has revealed a great deal of skepticism about the claims made by leading brands. That's true even though the companies making those claims may be quite well respected because of their size, longevity, and marketplace prominence.

Gallup has developed and tested a set of interrelated rating scales that, taken together, provide a reliable indicator of the Credibility that prospective consumers on first dates associate with a brand. Belief in a brand's commitment to keep its promises requires more than that the promises come from a trusted source; it also means that consumers must have a clear idea of what those promises actually are.

The four "Credibility" scales are:

✦ [Brand] is a name I can always trust.

✦ [Brand] always delivers on what they promise.

✦ [Brand] is a highly respected brand name.

✦ I know what [Brand] stands for and what makes them different.

A quick peek into the world of car buyers illustrates what an automaker must confront when attempting to overcome a prospect's doubts or even cynicism. Only about a third of potential auto buyers agree that they can always trust major carmakers' claims. Even fewer feel that the major brands always deliver on what they promise, even though a majority are of the opinion that the major domestic and imported makes are well-respected brands.

Our research reveals that about two-thirds of all prospective car buyers begin listening to an automaker's brand message with a strong degree of skepticism. They're uncertain whether the brand is likely to keep its stated pledge. That's not a great platform for a first date.

The very same situation exists for fast-food marketers, though getting stuck with a mediocre burger is far less onerous than being saddled with a Yugo. Only about 4 in 10 fast-food consumers say they can trust the blandishments of the major fast-food chains. And though about half feel that the national chains are highly respected brand names, far fewer agree that they always deliver on what they promise. Non-customer or first-date prospects are generally dubious that fast-food brands are both committed to their promises and capable of delivering on them. And in spite of the many millions spent to convince these consumers otherwise, that obstacle remains.

In each of the categories, a majority of prospects simply don't believe — however loudly, frequently, or creatively the brand message has been conveyed — that brands can always be trusted to deliver on their promises. And that's true despite high levels of brand recognition or a general regard for the company's business success. When the brand proposal is heard but not trusted, the prospects for a first date are bleak.

FUZZY PROMISES

There's an important reason why consumers may not assign much Credibility to the promises that companies make. That's because they simply don't know what those promises *are*. And the fault lies with the companies, because a surprising number do not (or perhaps cannot) articulate what their differentiating promise is. "Buy me" is not a brand promise, nor is "Shop here," "Stay here," or "Bank with us." That's a hope or a goal, perhaps, but it's certainly not a promise.

In various product and service categories, research reveals that though consumers may have seen and heard a brand's advertising, they still don't feel they can identify what makes the brand different. Regardless of the category we've examined, we often find that less than half of a brand's key prospects feel comfortable that they know what the brand stands for and what differentiates it from other brands. Therefore, they feel they're in no position to accept or trust the brand's offer.

The Credibility hurdle snags many brands well before they're able to attract that very first date. Yet there are two more hurdles that must be overcome for brands that hope to establish new relationships.

MOVING ON UP: PROMISES WITH PERSUASIVE POWER

A brand promise with Credibility still confronts a second major challenge. The promise must be *Compelling*. Consumers must feel that the brand offers a tangible return on their personal investment. Promises may be credible, but trivial. "We'll deliver it," though it's a believable promise, has considerably less potential for impact than "When it absolutely, positively has to get there overnight." The same applies to a statement like "We try" versus "We deliver."

Gallup's research among brand prospects has identified a set of four correlated items that together provide an indication of how Compelling — how powerful and persuasive — a brand's promise is. These items are presented as rating scales that reflect perceptions of the distinctiveness of the brand's promise, the degree to which it appears to attract other committed customers, and the nature of its marketplace presence. The four scales are:

+ [Brand] sets the standard for all other brands to follow.

+ There is no other [product/service category] quite like [Brand].

+ I can't imagine a world without [Brand].

+ [Owners/Buyers/Shoppers/Customers] rave about how great [Brand] is.

Together, these four ratings reveal the degree to which prospective buyers and users feel that a brand is likely to deliver — not just promise — the consistently outstanding performance that creates enduring brand relationships.

Brand-promise Credibility is difficult to achieve, but ensuring that the promise is Compelling is even tougher. When it comes to the auto industry, for instance, we find that only about a third of prospects believe that the promises made by the automakers are truthful. Less than half as many feel that those promises represent something meaningfully persuasive: That means that fewer than one in six prospects feel that any one of the major auto brands stands apart in any way from its competitors. Most prospects (more than 80%) aren't convinced that any of the major auto brands represent something that's meaningfully different. Has any company convinced prospects that there's nothing else like the car they're marketing? Only 14%-19% feel that way.

This problem isn't faced by a single auto brand; it's an epidemic. Each major automaker confronts a skeptical consumer audience that feels largely unmoved by any of the messages they've received. If a key role for a brand involves perceptual differentiation, then the overall conclusion must be: This job has *not* been accomplished.

And what we've seen for auto buyers holds true for consumers of every other product and service category we've researched. Marketers face not only the problem that consumers are skeptical, but also — no doubt because they've missed the Credibility hurdle — that the brand's intended differentiation message has failed to register. Whatever amount marketers are spending on designing and delivering brand communications, whatever media mix they're employing, a large chunk of prospective buyers is either ignoring or rejecting the company's brand message.

THE PERSONAL CONNECTION

The final test is even tougher. To generate a meaningful initial relationship, a brand promise must not only have Credibility and be Compelling, it must also personally *Connect* with consumers.

A personal connection enables prospects to readily envision themselves as brand customers — not just one-time purchasers, but regular users. Establishing this kind of connection requires more than simply meeting consumers' rational needs, such as promising quick service to a busy consumer or promising low-fat entrees to shoppers who are watching their cholesterol intake. Consumers have emotional needs, and meeting them is every bit as important — if not more so — as meeting their rational needs.

Our research has identified two related items that indicate the degree to which prospects feel a brand's promises are relevant enough for them to establish a personal connection with the brand. These two rating scales are:

✦ [Brand] is the perfect [product/service category] for people like me.

✦ I can easily imagine myself as a [Brand] [owner/shopper/buyer/customer].

A great many brand promises are overlooked or ignored because they lack Credibility. They also fall short when it comes to delivering a convincing and Compelling argument for change — something that motivates consumers to think of the brand as being apart from the ordinary.

Beyond these shortcomings, however, we've also found that most brands don't give consumers a sense that the brand speaks to them personally: "That's me!" And if consumers cannot see themselves as users — and proud, even delighted, customers — the prospects for a brand relationship are dismal.

Brand promises that are Credible, present a Compelling offer, and manage to personally Connect will attract first dates. But far more than that, they will generate a special type of first date — one that sets the stage for a continuing brand relationship.

However, only when "promises with potential for passion" are actually *kept* — at every subsequent encounter — does this initial date blossom into a fully engaged brand marriage.

Marketers could easily ask: If it's so difficult, why bother? And too many companies, it seems, reach that conclusion. Rather than attempting to convince a skeptical audience that their brand offers something truly meaningful and distinct, some companies have found it easier just to bribe their prospects. After all, giving the product away can also generate a first date, right? Deep discounts, coupons, free trials, rebates, and 0% financing have all been tried, and all are in regular use today. That's because they can move sales volume, at least over the short term. Repeat purchases that are driven solely by brand bribery, however, are not the same thing as a brand relationship.

CHAPTER SIX

FIVE Ps: TOOLS FOR THE BRAND-BUILDING TRADES

We know that Dell sells computers directly to consumers, bypassing intermediate distributors and retailers. They've obviously become quite successful at it, with more than $40 billion in yearly revenue and over 17% of the total world market in computers.

But what keeps Dell's customers coming back? It isn't the customized systems it builds, or the speed of the Internet for placing and fulfilling orders. It isn't even the cost savings that come from eliminating price markups from intermediate retailing channels. All of these factors contribute, but what keeps Dell's customers coming back isn't hardware, software, systems, or even prices. It's Dell's *people.*

We talked with Megan, who shared her story about her relationship with Dell:

> "My husband is a computer fanatic and changes things on the computer constantly. I'm always saying, 'What did he do now?' So I just call up Dell and say, 'OK, my husband's gone on this trip and I can't get into my computer. What do I do?' They are just so helpful when I call. Actually, there's this one guy that I call, and he knows me by name by now, which is kind of scary that I've called that often. But he's like, 'Oh, is this Megan?

> How are you? What's the problem? What'd your husband do?' He knows my husband now. I just couldn't live without them."

For Megan, Dell's people have turned a faceless retailer into an irreplaceable part of her life.

We also talked with Jim, another Dell customer who has a different feeling for the company:

> "It was so frustrating. I had a problem with a credit charge I thought was unfair, and there was nobody who could answer my questions. I was a loyal Dell customer who had bought three machines from them. I was furious, but they wouldn't even let me close my account over the phone. Some woman ... told me she couldn't give me credit, and she couldn't close my account. I would have to call back and try to speak with a supervisor. That's the last Dell product I ever buy."

Dell's products, prices, and delivery mechanisms were the same for Megan and Jim, yet the people component clearly was not. The result for Dell is two dramatically different brand relationships: one a marriage, the other a divorce.

MOVING FROM FOUR Ps TO FIVE

In their efforts to build great brands, companies have traditionally relied on a set of tried-and-true marketing tools. However, it appears that many of these companies are overlooking or ignoring what may well be the most important relationship-enhancement tool in their marketing toolbox.

The conventional implements contained in a brand marketing kit are well known and have been explored and dissected for some time. In graduate MBA programs over the past half century, they have been referred to as the "four Ps" — Product, Place, Promotion, and Price:

✦ *Product* encompasses whatever the company is attempting to market to consumers, whether it's a hotel stay, a mortgage, a microprocessor, or a box of laundry detergent. Product includes the brand name and product design, as well as the product features, the packaging, and even the warranty policies that might be included.

✦ *Place* concerns the manner, methods, and channels used to deliver these products to a consuming audience. Place includes the grocery shelf where products appear, as well as the fleet of delivery trucks, the location of a fast-food marketer's outlets, the exterior and interior design of a retail bank's branches and, more recently, the marketer's Web site.

✦ *Promotion* includes the broad range of communication activities designed to call attention to a company's offerings and deliver its message. Promotion encompasses mass-media advertising, direct mail, sponsorships, public relations activities, telemarketing, Internet pop-up ads, and any number of promotional events, all of which are "brought to you" by the brand.

✦ *Price* represents whatever the consumer is asked to pay to obtain the provided product or service and how that payment might be made.

These four Ps are the marketing tools that have been used to build great brands ranging from Ivory to Kodak to Coca-Cola. They've been discussed for decades. They've worked in the past, and they should continue to work — except that the world has changed. This change isn't just the result of the Internet, which can rifle messages to consumers at top speed. It's also a reflection of the growing importance of service industries in today's marketing arena. Companies don't just make products. Increasingly, they provide *services*.

And service involves an essential "fifth P," and its power often overwhelms the impact of any of the other four. This fifth P is *People*. The people that represent the brand may interact with consumers in person; they may be voices heard on the phone, or perhaps they're just names signed at the bottom of an e-mail responding to a customer request. They're the people who take customer orders, handle problems, fulfill a request, process a checkout, or simply greet an arriving shopper. They live the brand and, in the eyes of many customers, they *are* the brand.

BRAND BUILDING AND THE FIFTH P

Once the first date has taken place, customers are confronted with an important personal decision: to stay, or not to stay? Customers are called on to reconsider and perhaps renew their relationship. And every day, they face the ongoing overtures of competing brands that ask them to terminate existing relationships and start new ones.

In light of this, what can a company do to ensure an enduring brand marriage?

We can learn by listening to Sue, who described her disappointment when buying furniture from a local retailer. Sue didn't bemoan the color, the quality of the fabric, or the comfort of the cushions. Rather, she talked about the people who were called on to deliver on the store's brand promise — and who failed:

> "We bought furniture. Paid cash for it, which I thought was pretty good. They had it delivered. Ripped it bringing it through the door, then turned around and told us their delivery people weren't working directly for their furniture company. So we had to deal with them, and call and call and call. And I would get disgusted, told them to pick up the furniture. And they said we'd have to wait weeks to get our check back, and it would be hard to reorder."

Brand relationships and non-relationships result in no small part from the daily activities and responses of employees who serve as brand ambassadors and promise keepers for the company and to its customers.

PEOPLE POWER

In one comprehensive set of consumer studies, we talked with buyers and users of branded products and services ranging from fast food and airlines to long-distance telephone service and autos. There's a degree of service involved in each of these categories, and customers usually have some contact with people who represent the brand. Each category is characterized by intense competition among well-recognized brands that aggressively market to a broad audience. Thus, they represented an opportunity for us to look at all the elements of a complex mix of marketing tools in action.

In investigating these various categories, we asked customers about the brands they own, do business with, or use most often. We asked them about their purchase intentions and plans, and about their brand's advertising, product quality, value for the money, locational convenience, and accessibility. But the researchers looked beyond the traditional four-P marketing mix elements and asked about the people

— the fifth P — who served them when they bought or used the brand's products or services.

SECRETS OF SUCCESS: BEYOND TABLE STAKES

There is no single route to guaranteed success for any brand. But brand marriages that rely on a single marketing tool — whether that is Product, Place, Price, Promotion, or People — are as unstable as one-legged stools.

In part that's because competitors can readily copy almost any brand's product attributes, promotional approach, or distribution method. They can match prices, imitate product designs, and duplicate product features. The traditional four-P brand characteristics can quickly become table stakes.

But it's also important to remember that consumers don't encounter brands one "P" at a time. Any brand involves a combination of all five factors. In the words of one Old Navy enthusiast from New Jersey:

> "Old Navy [is] the perfect brand for me. Every time I go there, I have a good time. I enjoy the music in the background. The people that are there are friendly. They're really helpful when you're trying on clothes, and getting clothes for you. And the clothes are fun. It's practical, it's affordable, and they've added a section in the front that has more stylish and more dress–up clothes."

For this customer, as for many others, her relationship with Old Navy is a result of all five Ps, not merely one. And, as Gallup researchers noted in their summary of the fifth-P investigations:

1. Great Places cannot by themselves ensure the continuity of a company's customer relationships. An attractive store in a convenient location, kept clean and well lighted, is a great marketing asset. But it's not enough.

2. Great Prices alone, despite the abundance of price promotion evident in so many categories, are never enough to cement a continuing customer relationship. An attractive price is great, but it cannot build a relationship if it's combined with inferior products or mediocre service.

3. Great Products, in contrast with some marketers' stated beliefs in the overwhelming power of their products, also aren't enough. Valuable, yes. Sufficient, no.

4. Great Promotions, despite how much money is invested in support of advertising, sponsorships, and promotional events — and regardless of how visible and high-profile they may be — aren't capable of ensuring an enduring customer connection. Outstanding advertising is hardly commonplace, but even a great ad campaign cannot ensure a continuing relationship when the ads make promises that the products and people don't keep.

5. Even great People can't create lasting customer relationships if they are providing shoddy or overpriced merchandise.

WILL SOMEONE PLEASE HELP DENNIS?

Dennis visits a local sporting goods store on Saturday morning, intending to buy a ping-pong table he saw advertised. It's the exact table he wants, and the ad listed it at a great price. It should be a quick trip — he's preparing for a barbecue he's hosting that evening. Unfortunately, he can't find anyone to help him in the store, as the employees are all clustered about the store manager, who is regaling them with stories and lectures — probably about the need to be customer-focused.

Dennis waits for someone to notice him. He walks around the store, looking for assistance. He's not alone in that quest, as there are other customers who are also waiting for help. Dennis spots one employee who is stringing a tennis racket. He asks the person for help and is told he'll have to ask a sales associate on the floor. Dennis returns to the clustered associates.

"Excuse me. I hate to interrupt ..." he says.

The manager responds, "You'll have to wait. We're in the middle of something. Someone will be with you in a little while." But, 10 interminable minutes later, there is still no one available. While the manager is instructing the associates, the customers are being ignored.

Dennis leaves. He doesn't buy the table, and he never returns. Furthermore, he tells his story to the neighbors at his barbecue that evening, explaining why he hasn't been able to get the ping-pong table he hoped to have on hand to demonstrate his allegedly wicked backhand. Dennis mentions it at work on Monday, and he even e-mails his story to several friends in another city.

This store — and its manager — completely wasted a great opportunity to build a relationship with Dennis. This is a shame, because they had done everything they could from the boardroom and in strategy sessions to win Dennis' business. They established a convenient location, only a short drive from Dennis' home, and they stocked and offered a product he wanted, at a great price and prominently advertised. In this case, however, four Ps were not enough, because the store's performance on the fifth P was atrocious.

IT'S NOT JUST THE CAR, IT'S THE DEALER

In researching recent car buyers, we identified several important factors that affect repurchase and support an enduring brand marriage. In a survey of Ford owners, for example, we found those who rated Ford as "extremely" reliable were almost three (2.8) times more likely to say they would be buying another Ford when it came time for their next purchase. Chevy and Dodge owners who rated their vehicle brands as providing "extremely good" value for the money were, respectively, almost two (1.8) and three (3.1) times more likely to plan to buy another vehicle of that same make.

For Ford, Chevy, and Dodge owners — and for the owners of many other makes — Product and Price were important contributors to a continuing relationship with a vehicle brand. No surprise here.

Even in cases where products are obviously expensive, however, and where product quality and performance seem crucial, we found that Price and Product were *not* the number-one factors influencing a customer's repurchase intentions. Ford, Chevy, and Dodge owners who felt that the company's dealer representatives — the sales and service employees — "stand out" from all the rest were far more likely to indicate a strong desire to repurchase and repeat their ownership experience. Ford owners who were convinced that Ford's dealer-level associates stand apart were more than 13 (13.3) times more likely to indicate they would buy another Ford at the next opportunity. Chevy owners who felt the same way about Chevy's dealer reps were more than 12 (12.3) times more likely to say they'd be purchasing a Chevy. And Dodge owners who felt that Dodge's dealer reps stand out were almost 15 (14.6) times more likely to answer "Dodge" when asked about their next purchase.

Though People have a powerful impact on customers of these brands, Product is still important to auto buyers. For example, Ford owners who rated the reliability of their vehicle as "poor" were 20 times more likely to say they wouldn't consider buying another Ford.

Poor product quality is often the number-one factor in making non-customers out of customers, but consistent reliability is expected, even for domestic American cars. Reliability is table stakes. Marriages require something more.

As stated by Keith Crain, editor of *Automotive News*: "Reliability, real value for your price, real quality without any exceptions. Those are just the price of admission. ... But in the end, you must have something that creates passion in the mind of the buyer."

PEOPLE AND THEIR BURGERS

What's important to customers — and what keeps them returning time and again — is not necessarily what competing brand marketers trumpet in their advertising. It's also not necessarily reflected in how companies choose to allocate their marketing and brand-building spending.

In talking with regular fast-food patrons about their favorite brands, we found an obvious role for the product, the value it offers, and the convenience of the location. For example, one study found that McDonald's customers who prize the taste and quality of McDonald's food are almost twice as likely to indicate that they will return there when they next dine out. And customers who feel it's extremely easy to get to a McDonald's store are also more likely to return.

Though food quality and location are certainly important to a McDonald's customer, McDonald's People — the folks who are counted on to create the "smile" that's part of the brand experience — are of even greater significance. Customers who feel that the McDonald's employees who take the orders and serve the food are exceptional are more than five (5.1) times more likely to say they will hurry back. The same holds true for other fast-food restaurant brands: Burger King customers who feel their brand's store-level employees are superior are almost six (5.8) times more likely to return, as are Wendy's customers (5.5 times more likely to return).

For each of these leading fast-food marketers, our analysis revealed that the number-one driver of intent to return at the next opportunity is not the food, price, location, *or* advertising. It's the People. Does this mean that the taste appeal of the food is irrelevant? No. It means only that the food's taste is seen by many customers as being largely the same, at least when contrasting one large hamburger chain with another.

Customers aren't simply buying a Product at a Price. They are buying a total brand experience. That experience determines whether the first date leads to a second. And it determines whether dating leads to marriage.

CONTACT THAT BUILDS CONNECTIONS

We've found that customer-facing employees are critical to a healthy marriage whenever employees interact directly with customers. That's abundantly true in both business-to-business and business-to-consumer financial products marketing.

In our research among retail banking customers, the main driver of continued allegiance to the bank has not been the convenience of store location or access, nor has it been the cost of the checking account. These two factors, though they're often mentioned prominently in a bank's advertising, are viewed by banking customers as parity promises. They are table stakes. Though they're important, they don't differentiate one bank from another.

What does differentiate between banks is the People dimension. Employees and customer service representatives typically determine whether or not a bank's checking-account relationships are healthy. That finding is particularly interesting because many large banks have been pushing customers *away* from contact with the bank's People — into greater use of ATMs, online banking, and automated phone services — to reduce per-customer service costs. Our research indicates that by doing this, banks have actually minimized the potential impact of their strongest weapon for meaningful brand differentiation: their People.

THE DOORMAN'S FAVORITE ITALIAN RESTAURANT

Poor People-performance results in weak, vulnerable brand marriages — even when the company's Products offer some competitive advantages. But exceptional People can build exceptional brand relationships.

Jan and Pat are regional managers for a chain of retail stores. They were traveling together on business to Chicago and had decided to stay at a hotel that was new to both of them but located conveniently near the seminar they were attending. It also offered an attractive rate that fell within their corporate travel budget.

What attracted Jan and Pat to this Chicago hotel were the promises of a closer Place and a cheaper Price. In Jan's and Pat's experience, these promises set this hotel apart from its many competitors, which seemed about the same.

They were unfamiliar with the area around this hotel, so they asked the hotel's doorman about a good local place to eat. He suggested his favorite Italian restaurant. It was within walking distance, and he praised the food. "It's really great, but it's also pretty popular, so make sure you tell them I sent you."

It was very popular — and very busy — that Wednesday night, and Jan and Pat didn't have reservations. They were told there would be a 45-minute wait. Jan and Pat were disappointed, especially because, as they informed the restaurant manager, the hotel doorman had been really enthusiastic about several of their specialty items.

The manager told them, "Wait. I think I can help. There's another Italian restaurant, and it's not too far. Not quite as good as ours, of course," he said with a smile, "but very good. If you'd like, I'll give them a call."

"Great," said Pat, "where is it?"

The restaurant manager replied, "We've got a car. Our driver can take you there. It's no problem." The manager's car then took Jan and Pat to the other restaurant, where they were offered a free drink and enjoyed what they called a wonderful meal. "We were absolutely blown away by everything that happened," Pat said.

What about the hotel? In Jan's words, "It's an OK hotel. To tell the truth, it's really no great shakes, but it's certainly OK."

Would they return to the same hotel the next time they're in Chicago? "Absolutely. I'd look forward to it," Pat said, "because of that doorman. He was great. He mapped out a walking route for me, pointed out some great stores for shopping, and using his name got us great service at the restaurant." Pat added an even stronger endorsement: "We should hire him. He should be one of our store managers."

In most cities, there are many perfectly adequate, acceptable hotels; there are also quite a few acceptable and even enjoyable restaurants. What sets the exceptional ones apart are their employees and managers. Exceptional people build exceptional relationships — sometimes in just one evening.

HARNESSING THE POWER OF THE PEOPLE

People have a real and powerful role in defining a brand experience, which is why they are key to building successful brand marriages. But People are also the most difficult resource for companies to manage. The Fifth P poses the toughest challenge for marketing managers who strive to present a consistent brand image to the customer. Companies can make their hotels look the same and can ensure that the same advertising message appears everywhere. People, however, display a dramatic range in performance as brand "ambassadors."

But anything that is difficult for your rivals to duplicate can provide your company with the holy grail of brand building: a sustainable competitive advantage.

Obviously, all people aren't equally talented when it comes to connecting with customers. Some are great, but many are not. Few possess the ability to forge lasting relationships with customers. Those who can should be assigned to the most critical customer-facing roles — roles such as greeters, cashiers, tellers, call center representatives, flight attendants, and sales associates. These employees are brand builders — or at least they could be. Frequently, however, jobs like cashier, teller, or doorman are viewed as "warm-body" roles; these are the entry-level jobs from which valued and capable associates graduate.

Consumers don't regard these roles as irrelevant, however. To many consumers, entry-level employees *are* the company. Customers aren't greeted by Wal-Mart; they are greeted by and form an allegiance to Ramon or Margie. Customers don't get their coffee from Starbucks; they get it from Jayson or Shirlee.

Ritz-Carlton understands this better than most companies. It lives and breathes that knowledge, and it shares that understanding with others in its Ritz-Carlton Leadership Center seminars. One key topic in those seminars is "the power of empowering employees." For Ritz-Carlton, the customer experience is more than the breathtaking lobby, the luxurious down pillows, the health spa, or even the fluffy robes. The connection between a guest and Ritz-Carlton rises or falls as a result of its employees. Empowering its brand builders is just good business.

There's something else that brand managers should know: When it comes to building customer connections, it matters greatly how well the company's employees are managed. Gallup has done extensive research into "employee engagement," the degree to which employees are emotionally connected to the companies where they're employed.

Engaged employees contribute more. They stay loyal longer, and they're more productive. And, of critical importance, they also promote stronger and longer-lasting customer relationships. Simply put, *engaged employees help to produce engaged customers*. They build brand marriages. Disengaged employees, on the other hand, create disengaged customers. They stimulate separations.

There is a clear management lesson in all this. If People are important brand builders — as our research has consistently shown, and as company CEOs like Richard Branson (Virgin) and Howard Schultz (Starbucks) have attested — then management must make sure it puts its most talented people-connectors into customer-facing roles. And management must also take the steps necessary to enhance the engagement of its employees, because this has proven to be a critical ingredient for enhancing the engagement of its customers. For companies selling services, people are the marriage makers.

CHAPTER SEVEN

THE BRAND MARRIAGE: WINNING HEARTS AND MINDS

Happy brand marriages have a distinctive sound:

> "They always deliver. It always gets there on time. Always."

> "You feel like their people really care."

> "They've made a difference in my life."

> "I guess I'm addicted to them."

It's a sound in sharp contrast to that of a brand divorce:

> "I used to use them. I wouldn't be caught dead with them again."

Greatness, though it's certainly an enviable achievement, isn't necessarily an enduring one. Great brands can dwindle, losing all semblance of their former glory. Forty years ago, Schlitz beer was challenging Budweiser for marketing leadership in the United States, and Schaefer dominated the New York market. Today, Schlitz and Schaefer have essentially disappeared.

Each brand is called on to demonstrate its excellence not just once, but at every single brand encounter, every day. Inconsistencies in performance can, and will, damage the brand relationship. Customers will forgive an occasional slip, if they see it as an atypical performance-hiccup from a brand they otherwise love. But there's only so much goodwill in the forgiveness bank, even for a great brand; continual withdrawals will result in a depleted account and a spent brand relationship.

Great brands are those that manage to execute their brand promise consistently. They convey and support what some have termed a "package of value" for the consumer. That's a useful concept, but there are two important words included in this descriptive phrase: "package" and "value."

Offering customers a complete package may seem obvious, because no single characteristic can ensure an enduring brand marriage. However, the concept of value requires some additional explanation, because, when companies talk about value, they begin to sound like economists. They see value as some sort of algebraic formula in which the product's price is mathematically compared to the tangible customer need that it is intended to satisfy.

This formulaic emphasis on objective features and tangible needs typifies the way most companies conduct market research. Their researchers ask consumers about the "reasons" why they purchase — or don't purchase — certain products. Given this rationally focused approach, consumers' answers tend to dwell on the attributes, features, and rational benefits they receive. The following comments, gleaned from some of our consumer conversations, illustrate these responses:

> "If anything breaks, they'll replace it."

> "It's dependable."

> "It gets the whites very white, and the colors get clean."

> "They have well-trained people, and they back up the quality."

> "The sale items. And they have the selection."

> "They've been around for a while. They've stood the test of time."

> "It's a clean store, and the bathrooms are, too."

"Your satisfaction is guaranteed. There are no problems
with returns."

But consumers aren't computers, and their decisions aren't entirely
rational. If they were, life might be a good deal simpler for marketers,
and maybe a whole lot cheaper. Lipstick wouldn't be marketed for its
sex appeal and "kiss-proof" qualities. Nike probably wouldn't have
to hire Tiger Woods and Michael Jordan to convey what its clothes
look like and how its shoes perform. And Ferrari surely wouldn't be
tempted to market vehicles costing five times as much as a Honda and
with a reported top speed of almost 200 miles per hour.

Ferrari doesn't design its cars with the transportation needs of Los
Angeles commuters in mind. It designs its cars with their *dreams* in
mind.

LEFT BRAINS, RIGHT BRAINS ... AND WHOLE BRAINS

Marketers have long recognized, or at least suspected, that consumer emotions can come into play when purchases are made. Volumes
have been written about the importance of consumers' emotions. But
marketers have had mixed success in their attempts to manage these
murky feelings.

Emotions are often assumed to be a given. They're either magically
present in products, or they're not. For example, perfume is emotional,
but garden rakes are not. Vacation travel is emotional, but checking
accounts are not. Motorcycles and beer are emotional, but microprocessors and laptops are not.

This either/or dichotomy seems, on the surface, to fit the way consumers view products. Some marketing analysts have even extended
the either/or classification concept to consumers. They've drawn on
the work of educational psychologists to sort consumers into two
psychological categories: "left-brain" consumers, who are attuned to
linear, logical, concrete thinking, or "right-brain" consumers, who are
holistic, intuitive, symbolic. In other words, they're either engineers
or artists.

But that doesn't explain consumers like Tom, who says he doesn't
care about car brands, though many analysts contend that cars are emotional. Yet Tom isn't simply a left-brain decision maker in all areas. For
example, he feels emotionally tied to the brand of tea he drinks each
morning, roots passionately for his favorite baseball team, and has a

strong attachment to the restaurant where he dines with his wife on weekends.

The either/or dichotomy doesn't account for the Wells Fargo checking-account customer who is drawn to Wells largely because of its historical connection with the West and because it offers checks with a racing stagecoach printed on them. Nor does it explain the envious looks drawn by the person in seat 18C who pulls out the shiny, super-thin titanium laptop. And it certainly can't explain the appeal of the Nokia Vertu, a cell phone that can cost well over $10,000.

Our research reveals that emotions aren't merely a function of product category, but they're also not merely a function of a consumer's brain hemisphere dominance. Emotions vary, and they're enormously important — even though they've been elusive and difficult to measure and manage.

Whether choosing a brand date or committing to a deeper brand marriage, consumers are both left-brain and right-brain information processors. And though there are obvious differences between Nike and Dell, and between Disneyland and H&R Block, we've learned that *all* great brands have both rational *and* emotional connections with consumers.

That's not because brands are rational as well as emotional, but because consumers are.

EMOTIONS RUN DEEP

Listening to consumers and business-to-business customers talk about their brand experiences reveals not only the rational product attributes that impress them, but also their *emotional* reactions to the products and services they use. These emotional associations are critically important when it comes to understanding the brand relationship development process. Some of these reactions are positive:

> "There's a culture in that store. It's just a different attitude [they all have]."

> "I think it says something about me."

> "It just makes me feel great."

> "I feel stress-free when I'm there, and I enjoy myself, and it's very natural and soothing."

> "Not everyone is allowed to be a member, so it gives you an elite feeling."

And some of these comments, every bit as significant in determining whether the brand relationship will endure, reveal markedly negative emotions:

> "I had an unfortunate experience with them. It was traumatic for me."

> "I kind of really took offense."

> "I take it personally. I feel it's a direct insult. I get angry, and I tell others about it."

These comments also underscore what large-scale consumer surveys have shown: Consumers have both rational and emotional stories to tell about the brands they use, and they have both rational and emotional needs that they are seeking to satisfy.

THE SEARCH FOR LIFETIME RELATIONSHIPS

Business journals have featured numerous case histories highlighting the important financial payoff that comes from continuing, loyal, lifetime customers. Management consultants and researchers have reported that the longer a customer continues as a customer, the more profitable the relationship becomes. In his book *Loyalty Rules*, Bain's Fred Reichheld contends that an "increase in customer retention rates of 5% increases profits by 25[%] to 95%." Continuing customers usually spend more and, perhaps surprisingly, they typically require less. And study after study supports what has by now become a management mantra: It costs far more to replace a customer than it does to retain one.

However, for many companies, lifetime relationships remain an elusive goal. Customers arrive, then defect. They churn. And though companies may recognize that the foundations they've built with their customers have emotional as well as rational characteristics, this leaves them in a quandary. The rational underpinnings of a customer relationship lend themselves to precise measurement; emotional connections do not. As a result, many companies concentrate on the former while largely ignoring the latter.

Quantifying *rational* connections, such as brand attributes, is a simple, straightforward process. Market researchers merely ask consumers to rate the degree to which they associate certain attributes with a particular brand. How "refreshing" is Pepsi? How "comfortable" are Mazda's rear seats? How "reliable" is the home delivery service of the *Chicago Tribune*? How long was your wait for a bank teller?

In marked contrast, consumers' brand images and personality associations appear relatively soft. How "carefree" is Pepsi? How "confident" is Mazda? How "stimulating" is the *Chicago Tribune*?

Who cares?

Though various sorts of brand images and associations can be — and have been — measured, it's not clear why they should be. Companies need to be shown why these emotional associations matter, and the business payoff that comes from consumers' feelings about brands.

Because emotional associations have seemed elusive and fuzzy, and their ROI worth unknown, they have been largely relegated to the world of focus groups and exploratory research. Emotional outcomes have been difficult to quantify with the hard numbers demanded by CFOs and boards of directors. And thus the state of a company's emotional customer bonds has not been included as part of its balanced scorecard, and managers have not been held accountable for developing or nurturing those bonds.

However, that situation has changed. Emotional brand connections *can* be reliably measured. Even more importantly, emotional connections have been shown to link to a variety of financial payoffs, benefiting industries from banking to hotels, automobiles to frozen entrees, and industrial cement to pharmaceuticals. And these findings hold true not just for U.S. companies but for businesses in countries from Argentina to Thailand and from Germany to Singapore.

CRACKING THE CUSTOMER ENGAGEMENT CODE

In the summer of 2000, scientists at Gallup embarked on an ambitious and far-reaching R&D program to establish the ways in which emotional connections between consumers and brands could be reliably and validly ascertained. The aim was to provide a much-needed standard metric to quantify the emotional bonds that characterize a strong brand marriage. The program also sought to document the relationship between these so-called "soft" measures and important business outcomes, including customer retention, cross-sell, share-of-wallet, frequency of purchase, and profit per square foot.

A comprehensive list of candidate scales was pulled together, drawn from prior surveys as well as academic research into the psychology of human emotions. Customers in a number of product and service categories (new-car purchasers, recent fliers, and checking-account customers, for example) rated their current or most-often-used brand on a long list of measures. Following extensive analysis of these measures, a final list of items was selected based on their strong linkages to attitudinal loyalty and key business outcomes. This final list consists of 11 rating scales, called the CE^{11}. (For a complete list of these items, see Appendix B.)

The 11 individual scales have all shown an ability to predict business results. But there are some important interactions between the items, and these greatly enhance our understanding of the ways in which brand marriages are formed and sustained. The CE^{11} measures are arranged in a hierarchy of brand attachment. They begin with a foundation — the essential core requirement for any enduring brand marriage — and end at an apex that represents the height of achievement for any brand — an irreplaceable position in the life of the consumer.

IN PURSUIT OF BRAND PASSION

The hierarchy of emotional connectedness, as revealed through Gallup's research, is represented in the graphic "The Pyramid of Brand Attachment."

THE PYRAMID OF BRAND ATTACHMENT

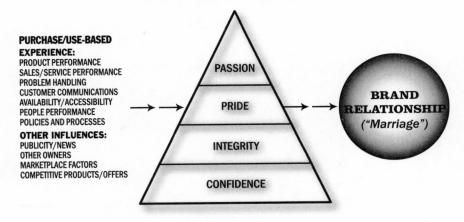

PURCHASE/USE-BASED
EXPERIENCE:
PRODUCT PERFORMANCE
SALES/SERVICE PERFORMANCE
PROBLEM HANDLING
CUSTOMER COMMUNICATIONS
AVAILABILITY/ACCESSIBILITY
PEOPLE PERFORMANCE
POLICIES AND PROCESSES

OTHER INFLUENCES:
PUBLICITY/NEWS
OTHER OWNERS
MARKETPLACE FACTORS
COMPETITIVE PRODUCTS/OFFERS

PASSION
PRIDE
INTEGRITY
CONFIDENCE

BRAND RELATIONSHIP
("Marriage")

As the pyramid reveals, emotional bonds consist of four related perceptual components that build to an overall emotional link that ties a customer to a brand. These four perceptual components are Confidence, Integrity, Pride, and Passion. Each is part of the overall emotional link that is forged by and shaped through the customer's ongoing experience with a company's products and services. And each of these four components can be reliably measured by a simple pair of rating scales.

Confidence and Integrity are the essential foundation for a brand marriage. They represent consumers' beliefs regarding a company's brand performance and its ability to keep its promises always, even when the going gets tough. There can be no real brand relationship if customers have doubts as to the brand's capacity or commitment to continue delivering on its promises.

Companies must address real or perceived performance shortfalls promptly, or they will erode the customer relationship. But there is more to a brand marriage than executing on the fundamentals.

Confidence and Integrity reflect consumers' beliefs about how a company treats buyers and users of its branded products and services. The next two levels of the "brand attachment" relationship hierarchy, Pride and Passion, reflect something even more important: how that treatment makes these customers feel.

CHAPTER EIGHT

KEEPING THE BRAND MARRIAGE VOWS
PART 1: BRAND CONFIDENCE

Brand marriages are grounded in the foundations of Confidence and Integrity, as shown below in the graphic "Brand Attachment: The Foundation." When the foundation is solid, the relationship is poised to continue. When it's shaky, the bond is in serious jeopardy.

BRAND ATTACHMENT: THE FOUNDATION

THE CONFIDENCE GAME:
THE FOUNDATION FOR A BRAND MARRIAGE

The bedrock of a brand marriage is Confidence, or the degree to which consumers have faith that a company is determined and able to keep its brand promise. If consumers believe that the company "tries," "does its best," or keeps its brand promise "most of the time," the company will fail to inspire Confidence. But if consumers are convinced that the company keeps the promises it makes to its customers, always and everywhere, consumers will have Confidence in the company or brand.

There is a world of difference between the consumer comments about brands that have generated brand Confidence ...

> "Amazon. They say it's going to be there in a couple of days, and it always gets there in a couple of days."

> "Continental Airlines. I always use them, especially for international travel, because they've always delivered ... in terms of comfort, safety, the luggage arriving, and just being consistent. I've always found that they carry through."

> "I've never had a bad meal there. I recommend them all the time."

> "They have what they say they're going to have. The manager says 'I'll get it for you,' and they do."

> "They have the 'Kid-Tough Promise,' where they say if a kid wears a hole in their pants before they outgrow them, they'll replace them. And they completely stand firm on that promise."

> "Coca-Cola is perfect. The taste is always the same. Way ahead of other sodas; it's the best. You always get the same thing over and over again."

... and the responses and reactions of consumers discussing brands that have, in their experience, failed to follow through.

> "This particular fast-food restaurant. You never know whether you're going to be the only one in line and still have to wait 15 minutes to get what you go for.

It's always a gamble. Is the food going to be accurate? I always have to check the bags."

"My local bank just got bought by a big, national bank … and it's a hit-or-miss situation most of the time. If I get one of the reps that used to be there, I'm pretty much assured of getting good service. If I get one of those corporate-trained people, it's … I might as well not be there."

Quantitative survey results reinforce these differences. Competing brands are almost never equally successful in generating consumer Confidence, because they're not as good at keeping their consumer covenant.

Because Confidence represents an emotional connection that is formed and earned over time, high levels of brand Confidence don't appear overnight or as a result of a first brand experience. Confidence evolves as a result of multiple brand encounters or dates in multiple venues.

We've also found that the customer covenant is endangered unless there is a very high degree of trust and faith in the company's commitment to the brand promise. Looking across a variety of product and service categories, a customer's expressed loyalty to a brand plummets an average of 29% when the customer's Confidence rating is anything less than superior (that is, a 5 on a 5-point scale). Negative business consequences result not just from poor, unacceptable performance but from any level of promise-delivery that customers perceive as being less than *great*. When it comes to customer Confidence, good is indeed "the enemy of great."

We've found that determining just how much real Confidence a company has established requires more than simply asking consumers how much they trust a brand. A meaningful measure must do more than sound like it measures what we think it should. It must reliably relate to hard-number business outcomes such as sales volume, cross-selling, and company profit performance.

CONFIDENCE: MEASURES THAT MATTER

Confidence can be measured reliably and efficiently through a simple pair of rating scales:

✦ [Brand] is a name I can always trust.

✦ [Brand] always delivers on what they promise.

Note that both of these measures use the word "always": Do customers feel that the brand always delivers and that it can always be trusted? Lukewarm agreement with these items is essentially valueless. Confidence requires strong agreement with both. Marriages aren't firmly grounded when the belief is that the spouse can "often" be trusted.

Together, these two ratings reflect degree to which customers feel the company and its representatives — including its products, services, and people — are succeeding in their efforts to deliver, not just that they are making an effort. When we've used this measure for products and services around the globe, we've found considerable differences between the levels of Confidence that customers ascribe to various brands. In the cases where we've found no differences, it's because all brands in that category are making the same promise and performing at parity in delivering on that promise. In short, if no differences exist, the brands have become undifferentiated commodities.

For an example, we need look no further than Detroit. In a survey of recent car purchasers in the United States, we found that only about one in four (23%) of those who had bought a domestic nameplate vehicle such as Ford, Chevy, or Dodge had high levels of Confidence in the company that made the vehicle. The rest of the car owners expressed some doubt about their car company's ability to always keep its consumer commitments.

In clear contrast, one in three (33%) of those who had purchased a car with an import nameplate like Toyota, Honda, VW, or Volvo expressed high Confidence in their car company. That's a considerably higher percentage than for the domestic makes — and as sales numbers would attest, this difference has real business consequences. Yet it must also be noted that two-thirds of import buyers also have doubts about whether their car company can always keep its promises. This points to a clear opportunity and a need for *all* car companies to increase their customers' Confidence in the brands they own.

Airline customers also have doubts. In our study of U.S. air travelers, we found that a third (33%) of one major airline's customers had a great deal of Confidence in the airline's determination to always keep its promises, compared to 1 in 25 (4%) of its competitor's customers. And Confidence matters outside the United States, too. Gallup found that 13% of German shoppers had Confidence in the retail chain where they bought many of their household products, while well over a third of their competitor's shoppers (36%) had Confidence in *their* chain.

It's easy to guess which of these brands were prospering ... and which ones were suffering.

A high degree of trust in the brand and in the brand's capacity to consistently deliver on its core performance pledge at every brand encounter is neither easily nor quickly achieved. Most companies regularly struggle with this, so it's often what differentiates the great from the merely good. But more must be done before the brand marriage can be considered truly healthy.

CONVEYING CONFIDENCE

Needless to say, building Confidence requires different performance actions from a financial services institution than from an auto dealer, a soap maker, or a clothing retailer. But despite the obvious differences, there are some important similarities in keeping the brand promise.

Confidence doesn't just come from the quality and reliability of a company's products. It's also conveyed by every customer encounter that reinforces the company's brand promise. Thus, Confidence is also built by a company's people, its stores, and its customer communications — from delivering all five Ps at every point of meaningful customer contact.

In banking industry studies, for example, we've found that Confidence doesn't stem only from a bank's painstaking attentiveness to detail and its unfailing accuracy in performing customer transactions. Banks understandably spend considerable effort in this area, and it's important. In one study, we found that customers who felt their bank was absolutely reliable and accurate in all its services were 24 times more likely to express Confidence in the bank. Customers who felt that their bank's employees were exceptionally friendly and helpful, however, were even more likely to be Confident: Customers who rated their bank's employees as exceptional were 28 times more likely to be

Confident in the bank. A bank's tellers are money in the Confidence bank — they're every bit as essential in delivery on the brand as are error-reduction systems and processes.

Similarly, car owners have a great deal of Confidence in their vehicle when it has been proven — to them, not just to *Consumer Reports* or J.D. Power — to have outstanding reliability. But they are almost equally impressed by dealer sales and service reps who appear highly knowledgeable.

In short: *People build brands* — at least the right people do — and they do it in part by reinforcing customer Confidence. They are major contributors in services where the product is a "smile," as might be the case with hotels, restaurants, travel services, and entertainment products. But they are also key contributors when customer expectations are accuracy and dependability, as in financial, telecommunications, and business services.

What's more, the combined impact of the various Confidence drivers doesn't merely add up — it can have an exponential effect. Below-average performance on just one aspect can actually outweigh all other positive, above-average performance factors. A computer program that consistently crashes, a bank that is subject to a scathing exposé on "60 Minutes," or a surly, uncaring flight attendant, can completely negate all of the other Confidence-building activities and costly initiatives the company may have implemented to build healthy brand relationships.

CHAPTER NINE

KEEPING THE BRAND MARRIAGE VOWS PART 2: BRAND INTEGRITY

The next level of the pyramid of emotional connectedness is Integrity. Like Confidence, brand Integrity reflects consumers' beliefs about how the brand performs. But Integrity goes a bit further, revealing a customer's feeling that the brand will always find a way to come through, even when "the going gets tough." If it's to continue, any relationship demands performance on rough seas as well as smooth. Brands with Integrity have customers who are firmly convinced that the company always keeps its part of the relationship bargain — and always will.

These consumer comments highlight the nature of these Integrity associations.

> "The Craftsman line of tools — they really stand behind their products. And the warranty — you know if anything ever breaks, they'll replace it for free."

> "I've never had anything bad that would even cause me to question them. I know I could always take something back if I had to. That's why I shop there."

> "I would cut this company some slack if they're having a bad day or if something just doesn't go right, because

in the end they'll make it right. Everybody makes a mistake, but I also expect service and responsibility for their actions. As long as they do that, we're all OK."

"My Internet service provider is like a small local operation. Unlike some of the corporate giants, I'm able to talk with customer service one-on-one, and get immediate attention whenever I have a problem. Those occasions are actually few and far between."

But we've found that Integrity is reflected not just in consumers' feelings about how companies will back their products and overcome problems, but also in the extent to which each customer feels treated fairly. When brands have Integrity, customers believe they can always expect to receive a fair return on their "investment."

"I put myself in that person's place. If like that person is treating me how I would treat that person … then that person is treating me fairly."

"I know I'm being treated fairly if I see the same quality of service being given to me as being given to others."

"A business owes a customer good service. The customer may not always be right, but a customer is still a customer."

"It's important to show that you value us as customers. You owe it to your customers to at least respond."

"The golden rule should be followed."

"It shows they deserve your business."

It's inevitable: Performance hiccups will occur sometime during the customer/company relationship. But quantitative surveys reveal that there are huge differences in customer perceptions of how well companies recover from these inevitable slip-ups, and there are large variations in the extent to which customers feel they're being treated fairly.

INTEGRITY: MEASURES THAT MATTER

Gallup's investigations have shown that Integrity can be reliably assessed through two intercorrelated rating scales. The scales used to measure Integrity mirror the nature of the contact that a company has with its customers. For situations in which the company has some direct person-to-person contact with its customers — whether that's over the phone, via the Internet, or face-to-face — these rating scales serve as capable detectors of brand Integrity:

✦ [Brand] always treats me fairly.

✦ If a problem arises, I can always count on [Brand] to reach a fair and satisfactory resolution.

The measures don't relate to whether companies are "doing their best." Instead, they emphasize demonstrated performance excellence — always. In this world of customer report cards, it appears that most brands get either an A or an F.

These two rating scales have proven to work well for products and services ranging from automobiles to pharmaceutical companies to resort hotels.

In situations where the company's contact with its customers does not include direct human contact, however, the Integrity metrics should be adjusted to account for that difference. Companies that market toothpaste, motor oil, laundry detergent, or software only rarely have direct personal contact with their end-users. Yet they may have plenty of important direct personal interaction with the distributors and stores that stock and display their products. These customers also must be courted.

For product marketers, their products are their brand ambassadors — but so are their packages, corporate policies, and multimedia brand communications campaigns. For companies that are product-focused, Integrity is measured through a pair of rating scales adjusted to account for the differences in how customers interact with the brand:

✦ [Brand] is a highly respected brand name.

✦ If a problem arises, I can always count on [Brand] to stand behind their products.

Like Confidence, Integrity is a perception that takes shape and is earned over time. Integrity ratings are influenced by how a company and its products perform long-term in the marketplace and, to some extent, by how they contribute to society. Integrity is also affected by a company's policies, processes, and procedures, and by the initiative and talent shown by the company's representatives.

A company's commitment to stand behind its products is not just a phrase. How a company handles marketplace crises, such as product failures or recalls, gives clear testimony to its Integrity, and contributes greatly to consumer perceptions of the brand. When problems occur, according to our customer report cards, it appears that most brands receive a grade of either A or F for Integrity.

The well-known story of Johnson & Johnson's response to the Tylenol product-tampering episode in 1982 established a high standard for how a company should respond to a crisis, even a crisis not of its own making. After discovering that its product had been tampered with, Johnson & Johnson immediately pulled the product from the shelves — at great cost to the company. The product was not reintroduced to consumers until the company had created new tamper-evident packaging. And the company did so across the United States, not just in the local area where the problem had been noted. Ultimately, its business rebounded, accompanied by public accolades and enhanced goodwill in the business press.

But despite that lesson, not all companies have the resolve or resources to respond so decisively. Their first reaction is often denial: "It's not really a problem, and besides, we're not at fault." That response won't enhance brand Integrity, and it won't make the marriage stronger.

We've seen differences in Integrity ratings among product and service categories. For example, fewer than one in five (17.3%) recent fliers feel that the airline they fly most has a high degree of Integrity when it comes to resolving problems. Consumers generally have much higher levels (35.4%) of belief in the Integrity of the banks where they have their checking accounts, as might be expected. But they also evidence greater feelings of Integrity in the online merchants (26.4%) and the mass merchants (28.0%) with whom they do business. These merchants occasionally make errors and disappoint their customers. But when they do, consumers are likely to feel that the merchants they deal with — unlike the airlines they fly — will quickly take action to remedy performance glitches.

But overall percentages mask the enormous variation that often exists between brands. On the whole, the vast majority of recent fliers don't give their airlines high marks for fairness and Integrity. However, a few airlines *have* managed to buck this trend. These high performers generate feelings of Integrity among their fliers that are 2, 3, and 4 times — and in some cases, as much as 10 times — higher than the Integrity levels manifested among their competitors' fliers.

In another study that focused on grocery shoppers, 4 in 10 (40%) customers of a grocery chain felt their chain had high Integrity, but more than half (56%) of their competitors' customers felt that way about their chain. In a study in Latin America, the contrast was even greater: 40% of a grocery chain's shoppers felt assured that their chain would treat them fairly and with Integrity, while a mere 7% of a competitor's shoppers felt that way about their store.

We can draw an important conclusion from these results. Though some companies greatly outperform their competitors and benefit from that performance, consumers feel that most companies fail to meet a standard of excellence when it comes to reducing and resolving problems.

This is significant, because we've found in our research that unless problems are handled *at excellence*, the customer relationship is in jeopardy. To customers, the company's response to their problems and frustrations is the acid test of its commitment to serve them. It powerfully demonstrates the extent to which the company lives its customer promises.

THE GOLDEN RULE

It's important to note that treating customers fairly should not be confused with special treatment. Though customers may be delighted by being singled out for extraordinary benefits and perks, they expect to be treated equitably. They expect rewards commensurate with their level of support for the company and its products.

Thus, frequent fliers expect more than infrequent fliers do because they feel they've earned it. Larger and longer-term business customers expect treatment that acknowledges the depth and length of their relationships — and they don't want to receive a level of treatment that seems inferior to what others are getting.

As Helen states it:

> "I know I'm being treated fairly if I walk into the store, or if I ask for a particular service and I see the same quality of care being given for me as for others. It really bothers me when I walk into a store, and I stand there, and no one comes to assist me, but then someone else will walk in and there will immediately be one or two people there."

Others echo Helen's sentiments and emotions, relating stories about fair (or unfair) treatment — and why that makes a real difference to them:

> "I feel that the golden rule should be followed. If someone treats me unfairly, I feel it's a direct insult to me. I shouldn't feel that way, but I do. And I tend to get angry and tell others about it."

> "I want to be treated the same as others. Sometimes assumptions are made about someone's looks, and I try to avoid stores like that."

> "I cut them some slack. Everybody makes a mistake, but they [need to] say they're sorry. And in the end, I know they'll make it right."

> "I expect a store to stand behind their products. That shows they deserve your business."

> "I feel I'm being treated fairly when I feel like I'm being listened to and my concerns are being heard. Whether or not my needs are met, I take a great deal of satisfaction from knowing that I was at least listened to and heard."

Again, Integrity doesn't imply a perception of error-free performance. Instead, it strongly suggests that:

+ errors and problems will be rare rather than frequent, and
+ identified problems will be acknowledged, handled, and equitably resolved

Customers want to feel validated and appreciated, and they expect to have their feelings acknowledged and their relationships recognized.

Some companies use customer relationship management (CRM) programs to facilitate that recognition. These programs provide comprehensive, computerized customer-tracking systems that can identify and flag customers according to the level, length, and depth of their relationship. Unfortunately, these programs are seldom used to express appreciation, recognize customers, or reinforce the customer relationship. Far more often they're simply a mechanism to try to sell customers more stuff. Marketers, take note: Inundating current customers with a mailbox full of new offers doesn't enhance their perceptions of brand Integrity. Instead, it screams of a company's self-interest.

Though companies contend that they require all customers to be treated fairly and equitably, their marketing programs may not support this. Consider the marketing efforts of many banks, credit card companies, phone services, and newspapers. Newspapers often offer deep discounts on their prices or charges, but only to new customers — not to the loyal subscribers who have been faithful readers for the past decade. Banks likewise ignore existing checking-account customers who have paid their monthly fees without complaint for the past 7 years.

Where is the "fairness" and reciprocity in this? Small wonder, then, that customers may perceive that their business is being taken for granted, or that they're being treated less well than customers who have yet to prove their commitment. Businesses that offer special deals for newcomers may gain new customers, but at the cost of disengaging their committed customer base.

PROBLEMS, PROBLEMS, PROBLEMS

How well does your business deal with your customers' problems? Your response to customer difficulties has an enormous impact on customer perceptions of your company's Integrity.

The overall health of the brand marriage can be severely affected by problems, whether large or small. We've found that the expressed loyalty of customers who have experienced a problem will typically decline by as much as two-thirds. Problems weaken the customer connection, eroding its foundation and causing buyers or users to doubt your brand's ability to deliver its promised performance.

Problems occur, and customers understand this. But when problems happen, how they are handled is actually much more important to customers than whether they are resolved. Although resolution is obviously important, it's possible for customers to get there without feeling that the company has Integrity. Resolution can be forced, as any tort lawyer will gladly attest — but dragging a company into court and winning a settlement isn't the way to build customer engagement and goodwill.

Research into problem-handling underscores the potential for relationship recovery even while it highlights the demanding nature of this challenge. Problems handled at excellence can, we've found, actually enhance the customer relationship. In these cases, the company's Integrity is reinforced or even bolstered by evidence of the company's real commitment to its customers.

However, only about one in seven customer problems are typically handled at excellence, our research reveals. What's more, anything less than excellence appears to be enormously destructive, placing the brand marriage in peril.

On the other hand, where excellence exists in problem handling, the relationship can emerge even stronger. Consider the following story, told by a New Jersey mother of three:

> "When one of my children was very young, she would put herself to sleep with a little lullaby toy, and that's how she learned to go to sleep. One night, it just stopped working, and I'm not sure what went wrong or why. I called the company's 800-number on the back of the product. I got a really nice woman who didn't say, 'Well, you know, you need to take it back to the retailer.' Instead, she said, 'I'll ship one out to you today.' There was no charge. She didn't ask me to send back the damaged product. She just took my word for it and sent me a new one. I was really surprised and very pleased."

That's not a typical company response, of course. Contrast that mother's story with the following tale of woe, told by a young mother in the Midwest:

> "They said they had a return policy. Well, I had the receipt. I had everything. And I took it back in, and they wouldn't exchange it. They wouldn't even give me anything for it. It was very upsetting because of what

they had told me — the saleslady. I had told her it was a gift, and that I was going to show it to the person, and if I brought it back would they exchange it or refund or give store credit. But when I came back that same salesperson wasn't there, and they wouldn't exchange it. They wouldn't do anything. They just said, 'Well, it's yours now.' I haven't been back since."

When problems aren't resolved or promises aren't kept, negative consequences follow. And even when the promise is eventually — and perhaps reluctantly — kept, the consequences are detrimental to the customer's emotional connection to the company. In a survey of the U.S. auto industry, about one in five (21.2%) car buyers said they had a problem with their vehicle recently. Some of these problems were more serious than others, but that wasn't the critical factor; to consumers, anything they say is a problem is something worthy of being addressed.

The customer engagement level of car owners who didn't have any problems was 3.6 times greater than the engagement level of those who did. Even more revealing was the impact of how well these owners' problems were handled. Fewer than one in five people who had a problem (18.4%) were extremely satisfied with how it was handled by the automaker or its dealers. When problems were handled at any level below excellence, customer engagement almost vanished, and the percentage of fully engaged customers sank to only 1.1%. These customers were *25 times* less engaged than those who never had a problem.

Our research has revealed similar results in studies of hotels, banks, grocery stores, airlines, and credit cards. Effective problem-handling is key to relationship recovery.

HANDLE WITH CARE

For several decades, companies around the world have been striving to eliminate problems, and those efforts have obvious merit. The focus on error-reduction and defect-elimination is perhaps most evident among automakers, where total quality management (TQM) has been the guiding mantra. The search for zero defects represents the grail for manufacturers in other fields as well, and it's the driving force behind Six Sigma programs.

Whenever humans are involved, however, there will always be problems — so the goal must be fewer problems. Thus, every company must have a relationship recovery program — one designed to effectively and efficiently handle problems, to minimize the emotional disconnect and divorce that could otherwise result.

When a problem occurs, companies should begin the relationship-recovery process by acknowledging that the customer actually has a problem. While this sounds simple, it's not regularly done; companies are leery of accepting responsibility, fearing it will pave the way for costly lawsuits. But acknowledging a problem doesn't mean the company accepts fault. It means merely that the company understands that there has been a disruption in the reciprocal relationship. It also helps the company address an important psychological need: Customers want the company to recognize and hear their concerns.

John Fleming, in his *Gallup Management Journal* article, "Sorry Seems to Be the Hardest Word" (see http://gmj.gallup.com), outlines six simple but essential steps toward relationship recovery:

✦ Acknowledge the customer's concern.

✦ Apologize, even it it's not clear who's at fault.

✦ Empower your staff to resolve common problems on the spot.

✦ Follow up if there's been no resolution within a certain time frame.

✦ Institute an automatic escalation procedure to ensure that even the most furious customers feel assuaged.

✦ Leave the customer better off than he or she was before the problem.

Confidence and Integrity are critical requirements for a continuing brand marriage. Because they exist only at "greatness," they are certainly not easy to achieve or to maintain. But they reveal how well a company is keeping its covenant and living up to its part of the brand bargain through the all-important eyes of the customer.

The next two steps up the brand attachment pyramid reveal just how this makes customers feel. And feelings of Pride and Passion ultimately define and determine the strength of the customer-brand connection and the real health of the brand marriage.

CHAPTER TEN

BUILDING ON THE FOUNDATION: BRAND PRIDE

Ensuring a solid foundation for a lasting brand relationship requires ongoing vigilance and a pervasive company-wide commitment to performance. Yet that's still not enough. As difficult as it might be to establish strong feelings of Confidence and Integrity in a brand, many more brands have reached this plateau and failed to scale the full height of the brand attachment pyramid. But every brand should strive to reach the top of that pyramid, as shown in the graphic "Brand Attachment: Building on the Emotional Foundation."

BRAND ATTACHMENT: BUILDING ON THE EMOTIONAL FOUNDATION

PRIDE VERSUS PRESTIGE

The first of these two higher levels of emotional connectedness is brand Pride. Pride is the extent to which shoppers, owners, or buyers feel good about their use of a brand; it's also whether they feel good about being a brand's customers and how it reflects on them personally.

There is much more to this emotional response, however, than the prestige-based badge value of a brand. Sure, people feel a good deal of pride in owning a Mercedes, flashing a platinum AmEx card, or wearing a Harvard sweatshirt. This type of public pride is reinforced by the esteem that others presumably feel for these brands. But customers also feel a private pride, and this is every bit as important (and powerful) as its more public counterpart.

We've observed considerable pride among consumers who buy value brands and shop at discount merchants that make their customers feel wanted, personally appreciated, and even treasured as smart buyers. Consumers have high levels of pride in buying brands that reflect, reinforce, and somehow complete their own self-images. These feelings are evident even when their purchases are neither visibly apparent nor readily recognizable by others.

We can hear the diversity of Pride responses in many consumer comments. These comments also provide a sense of the deeper emotional significance of these brand associations:

> "I'm known as the Rubbermaid Queen. It organizes my life."

> "When do I feel pride? When I walk out (of the store) knowing they want me back again."

> "I'm probably a walking advertisement for Eddie Bauer. It seems that everything I own looks or pertains to Eddie Bauer."

> "It's when I feel I'm being listened to, and heard ... like I'm a real person and not just customer X."

> "I feel really good about driving a Buick. Not that I think it's the most prestigious. I'm just proud to drive my Buick. I think it's beautiful. I even gave it a name: Maria."

The sense of personal attachment is often reflected in consumers' use of personal pronouns ("*my* Buick"; "*my* Miracle Whip"; "*my* Wal-Mart"); the brand is integral to their lives. It's part of them and part of what helps define them to the world they inhabit.

> "The only item I do not skimp on, for myself, being a former caterer. It's very important to me that I buy quality food items. That's who I am. I'm Aunt Pam, and everyone comes to my house for a great meal. And so, far be it from me to serve something under (that doesn't match up to my brands)."

> "I wear a Nike logo on my hat, proudly. I remember Nike back when I was little, and I'd wear Nike sneakers. It just brings back fun memories. So, I wear it proudly."

Consumers are deeply proud to be associated with brands that provide them a sense of reciprocity, a belief that the company values them — not as a number, but as a vital and much-appreciated individual.

To be real, this reciprocity must be deeply felt and genuinely expressed whenever the company touches customers. When Damien talks about *his* pizza place, he does so with considerable Pride. He mentions the product, the price, and the convenient location. But he also emphasizes the feeling he gets from the pizza shop's people.

> "There's a little mom-and-pop pizza shop around where I live. The quality of the food is excellent. The prices are extremely reasonable, and the service is not only reliable, but cordial and friendly. It kind of feels like I'm having a friend deliver my pizza, instead of a company. And they will get my money over any of the major pizza chains, any day of the week."

BRAND PRIDE: MEASURES THAT MATTER

Our analysis revealed two measures that reflect feelings of Pride. Both indicate the reciprocity and mutual respect that are essential to any relationship. As is the case for Confidence and Integrity, Pride is assessed through a pair of rating scales. They were selected not because they sounded interesting, but because they proved to reliably reveal the feelings and emotions expressed by consumers involved in brand marriage relationships.

The two measures of brand Pride are:

✦ I feel proud to be a [Brand] [customer/shopper/user/owner].

✦ [Brand] always treats me with respect.

These two items don't just reflect consumers' attitudes toward particular brands; they also indicate how consumers react to the brand experience and to the reality of their lives as brand customers. These are the feelings that matter.

Again, the measures require evidence of real "greatness" in a brand relationship. There is an important difference between customers who react by saying, "Yes, pretty much," and those who respond, "Absolutely!" Pride exists only where there is greatness.

WHERE THERE'S PRIDE

As with the "brand attachment" components, we see large differences between competing brands in the Pride felt by their buyers, users, and owners. What's more, Pride exists in every product and service category and in every consumer segment that we've examined. There's Pride in buying soap and ketchup and in purchasing software and laser printers, not just in owning a car or buying a tailor-made suit.

When it comes to automobile brands, we've seen brands that inspire almost 7 in 10 owners (68%) to point with great pride to their association with the brand and their experience as an owner. We've also observed competing brands that stimulate much less loyalty — where, even though consumers had spent well over $25,000 on a purchase, only 16% say they're proud to be an owner. That means that five out of six of this brand's owners aren't particularly proud of their association with the brand, despite the price they paid. That portends big problems on the road ahead: not only are unenthusiastic owners unlikely to be repeat purchasers, they're also less positive and more negative when talking with others about their cars.

Brand marketers have come to recognize the potential business-building — or business-killing — role of word-of-mouth brand buzz, brand advocates, and customer evangelists. Thus, Pride is important not just for what it means for the individual customer, but for what it implies for everyone with whom that customer comes in contact.

And the importance of Pride extends beyond the world of multi-thousand-dollar purchases. We've looked at grocery store chains where 4 out of 10 (41%) customers feel extremely proud of their store relationship. Yet in other chains, which sometimes have stores just down the block, only 19% of their customers feel proud to be known as customers. Guess which marriages are on the rocks?

In the financial services industry, there are banks that inspire more than a quarter (28%) of their customers to feel great Pride in professing their connection with their bank; in other banks, the percentage is just 12%. Which bank would you prefer to manage — and which one would you want to marry?

Pride is required for a strong and profitable brand relationship.

THE FEW, THE PROUD ...

Most brands don't create high levels of Pride among their customers, according to our research. Part of the reason is that most brands fail to create or define a unique brand experience that makes their customers feel special.

Marines feel a high degree of Pride, as do iMac users, Phish fans, and eBay aficionados. Their Pride is driven by the knowledge that they are part of a distinct minority, an "in" group of the initiated. They are connected to the brand and bonded to its other users as a result of the brand's special quality and the distinct nature of the brand experience.

There is an implied dilemma, which becomes evident as the brand expands its distribution in search of additional sales and income. What happens to a brand that is special and "not for everyone" as it strives to gain customers across a broader spectrum?

As a regional brewer, Coors had an intensely loyal following bonded to and very proud of the brand because of its unique, Colorado- and Rocky-Mountains-only availability and image. However, as Coors expanded to maximize its volume potential, it also lost a good deal of the Colorado panache that had cemented its original customers to what they saw as a unique, personal brand experience that was not readily available to or intended for all.

What will happen to brands like In-N-Out Burger or Krispy Kreme doughnuts as they continue to expand their availability? Will they still have the same appeal when customers don't need to go out of their way to find these limited-availability offerings? In-N-Out has approached its expansion cautiously, striving to ensure absolute consistency of the brand experience at every store. Krispy Kreme, in contrast, rapidly exploded across multiple domestic and even international markets, selling its products not just in its own stores but in grocery and convenience stores in many markets. Forgetting for the moment the management and accounting problems that the Krispy Kreme company faces, the real question remains: How far can its brand presence expand before it becomes "just another doughnut"? The Krispy Kreme brand experience isn't duplicated merely by expanding its product distribution.

Opening up brand membership can water down a brand's distinctiveness and detract from the exceptional Pride felt by its customers. How large can the membership grow before the group no longer has something singular and sharply distinct in common?

It doesn't have to be that way, though a loss of distinction is one potential outcome. Customers can feel Pride when affiliating with very large brands. Some brands' Pride levels are derived from maintaining small, cult-like clans of committed customers, while other broadly distributed, mass-oriented brands boast customers who are extremely proud of their brand relationship.

Starbucks seems to have maintained a good deal of its customer Pride despite greatly extending its reach and the number of its stores, which now number in excess of 7,000. The real question is whether it'll be able to continue to do so as it further expands its product — though not its total brand experience — into airplanes and hotel rooms and onto grocery shelves, right alongside Folgers and Maxwell House.

R.E.S.P.E.C.T.

One key is to recognize that the Pride component of the brand relationship isn't a result only — or even primarily — of limited availability and a sharply differentiated audience. A key aspect of Pride is a feeling of being valued, appreciated, and personally *respected* by the brand and its representatives.

Pride is a reflection not only of the pride felt by the customer, but also of the pride the company feels and expresses about its customers. Pride is, and must always be, reciprocal.

As one illustration of this, consider the comments made by Daryl, formerly a regular customer (and a proud one, to boot) of a major retail chain in the Eastern United States. Daryl's draft of a note to the company's management team tells a story well worth hearing:

> "Tell your salespeople not to sound like they're reading from a script. It seems that so many of the people who work there, and are supposed to help you, are disinterested in who you are. Even if they are [disinterested], at least give the appearance that you care about my needs and that you are willing to put some effort into helping me get what I want."

A company shows that it appreciates its customers' business and patronage through its policies, processes, products, and people. It does so at every point of customer contact and through every communication the customer receives. Respect for the consumer can come through in myriad ways. Famed ad-agency founder David Ogilvy once lectured his creative teams, "The consumer is not a moron. The consumer is your wife."

Pride demands something more than paying attention to basic customer-service fundamentals. It also requires something beyond corporate lip service or a hackneyed "customer-centric" mission statement that exists on the boardroom wall but isn't lived in the stores. Pride requires real, tangible evidence that a company values every individual customer and every customer relationship.

CHAPTER ELEVEN

THE EMOTIONAL PINNACLE: BRAND PASSION

Confidence, Integrity, and Pride constitute a brand edifice of which any CEO should be justifiably proud. Yet, as with every building, there are the finishing touches that separate the temporary from the permanent, and that represent the difference between a functional dwelling and a greatly cherished dream home. The difference between "like" and "love" in a customer relationship is Brand Passion.

Consumers who are passionate about a brand are convinced that it's absolutely perfect for them. Moreover, they've come to believe that their world would be somehow incomplete if that brand were no longer available.

There are products that seem irreplaceable. These include essentials, like refrigeration or antibiotics and other wonder drugs. They also include more mundane products and services that have carved out unrivaled niches in the everyday lives of consumers: The television remote, cell phones, microwaves, and e-mail fall into this category. We can't live without them.

However, brands also inspire Passion:

> "I couldn't live without ... Shredded Wheat. I have it every day. It's part of my daily routine, and without it my day isn't complete. It sounds silly, but when my

> husband went to eat the last bowl yesterday, I bit his
> head off."

> "Without that brand? I would feel as if I'd lost a good
> friend."

> "For me, it's Casual Corner. When I go there, they know
> who I am. I have a sense of comfort there, and I'm
> always happy to pick up the phone (when they call)."

> "Singapore Airlines. They have great customer service.
> Once, when I was sick, they took care of me. I felt
> really taken care of. They went the extra mile."

Even business-to-business customers express their passion for some
brands:

> "Frankly, I just don't know what we'd do without them.
> They've always been there for us. They don't just re-
> act to our emergencies, and we have plenty of those.
> They keep coming to us with ideas. I think they care
> as much about our success as we do."

Passion is at the apex of the brand attachment pyramid. It's the ultimate emotional bond for any brand, one manifested in the customer's
dedication to supporting and even evangelizing its merits.

While hardly widespread, brand Passion is evident in some surprising places. We've found it not only in the land of luxury vehicles
and resort hotels, but also in the presumably dispassionate world of
mortgages, gas stations, and packaged cheese. It's there, waiting to be
stoked — and to be understood.

Wherever there is brand Passion, there are also rival brands that
fall short of their competitors — and some that don't even come close.
These latter brands suffer as a result; they have weaker emotional links
with customers, and they're also vulnerable to the negative business
consequences that follow from a flimsy customer relationship.

CALL ME IRREPLACEABLE

Passion can be detected and monitored, and that paves the way for
how it can be *managed*. The metric for assessing brand Passion consists,
as with the other three components of brand attachment, of two related
rating scales:

✦ [Brand] is the perfect [company/product/brand/store] for people like me.

✦ I can't imagine a world without [Brand].

Time after time, customers show they can readily rate the brands they use on these two scales. That doesn't mean customers are passionate about lots of brands. They're not. It means only that their ratings are clear and consistent indicators of the extent to which their brand marriages are marked by a deep commitment — a sense of brand Passion — and not merely by convenience or habit.

Studies show that there are vast differences between competing brands:

✦ In a survey in India, almost a third (31%) of the buyers of one packaged food product had Passion for that brand. Their competitor generated Passion among only 22%.

✦ In a grocery shopper survey in the United States, one chain built brand Passion among just one in six (16%) of its customers but was attempting to compete with a chain that had achieved this same level of customer Passion with almost half (45%) of its customers.

✦ A leading U.S. insurance company had created Passion among one in five (22%) of its current customers, while attempting to compete with other companies whose levels of Passion ranged from 31% to 53%.

Insurance might not seem like a category that would be marked by much Passion. That's why many financial services products have been marketed like commodities. However, just because *companies* treat their products like commodities does not mean that *consumers* view them that way.

Consumers are passionate about the brands they feel are perfect for them — brands they feel they absolutely couldn't do without. The second component rating illustrates how consumers feel about this relationship: "I can't imagine a world without [Brand]." It sounds extreme, and it is. That's intentional, because we're searching for truly great brand marriages. This measure separates world-class performers from merely good ones; it distinguishes the passionate from the perfunctory.

We've found Passion in almost every product category. We've found it among rich customers and poor ones, among the old and the young, and among men and women. Business customers express Passion, as do individual end-users. We've found it in Thailand and Brazil, as well as in Germany, Japan, and the United States. In short: Passion is there, even if it seems invisible, and even if nobody has noticed until now.

STOKING THE FIRES OF PASSION

When researchers dug into what it takes to build brand Passion, there were three obvious conclusions:

+ First, the particular drivers of Passion vary by category and by brand. What passionately bonds a car owner to a BMW is not the same thing that forges relationships for Lexus, Jaguar, or Volvo owners.

+ Second, it's never just one thing, like the styling or the handling for an automobile. Not when we're talking about Passion.

+ Third, the key in every instance is differentiation — being meaningfully different in the signals and cues that tell customers that their brand experience is something unique and really special.

Research among recent fliers shows that Passion doesn't result from schedule convenience, memorable commercials, or the age and condition of the aircraft. Though these are relevant factors, they're not what creates brand Passion.

When it comes to airline customers, Passion stems first from exceptional people in the air, followed by exceptional people on the ground, and last, by dependable arrivals and departures. That's interesting, especially because that's precisely the performance profile pioneered in the United States by Southwest and now also pursued by carriers like Ryanair and JetBlue. Small wonder, then, that these newcomers have outperformed the larger airlines, which have had difficulties in their attempts to deliver a warm and welcoming brand experience. Small wonder, too, that the larger legacy airlines have had to rely on discounts, sales, and frequent flier programs to bribe their customers into returning.

When there are no people to serve as brand ambassadors, companies must rely on other factors to build brand Passion. But it can be done — and we've seen evidence of that fact, in ketchup, coffee, hand soap, and face cream. Passion derives from meaningful differentiation in the experience of using the brand, which is what brand greatness is all about: a truly unique flavor, as we found in a study of salsas in Latin America and a study of beverages in the United States; a distinct and refreshingly clean feeling, as we discovered in a study of bath products in Asia; or a uniquely satisfying experience, as we noted for a food product in India. To build customer Passion in any country, the brand experience must be uniquely different.

For products like ketchup and coffee, great advertising and distinctive packaging help frame and support the distinctive brand experience. Again, the fundamental requirement for Passion is greatness, not "good enough." Therefore, the marketing challenge is to create, communicate, and consistently reinforce a distinctly different feeling, one that can come only from buying and using — and from being married to — the brand.

But this requires understanding the total brand experience from the customer's perspective, not just the company's. Is the Starbucks brand experience the coffee, or something beyond that? Is the Starbucks experience replicated in the aisles of a United flight from Denver to Chicago — or is it just the coffee that's replicated?

The elements that signal a differentiated brand experience are often subtle. But they are crucial cues to the customer, because they're the aspects of the total brand experience that set it apart. In his book *Clued In*, Lewis Carbone addresses the need to identify the clues that trigger emotions. And in his recent book *Brand Sense*, Martin Lindstrom points out how each of the five senses serves a vital role in building the emotional associations that separate strong brands from weaker ones.

Companies can use a number of qualitative tools to probe the potential triggers of a customer's brand experience. But one key question remains: Exactly what emotions should the brand be triggering? Here's an answer: Confidence, Integrity, Pride, and Passion. Focus on the clues and sensory signals that convey these four, because these are the essential ingredients for a brand marriage.

Importantly, building Passion isn't just a challenge for the company's ad agency. It also confronts its product developers, store and package designers, flavor profilers, merchandising managers, process engineers, and everyone else involved in crafting and executing the brand experience.

Customers cannot simply be told that a consumption experience is uniquely pleasurable, regardless of how much advertising weight is placed behind "bite and smile" ad campaigns. A promise demands delivery. Customers must experience the brand's uniqueness. They must feel the difference — because emotions are all about feeling.

Identifying the subtle but important signals that reinforce the platform for brand Passion isn't a simple task. Neither is the creation of a unique product experience that consistently conveys those differentiating signals. It's all easier said than done. But there's no Passion without it, and marriages without Passion will drift ultimately, and sometimes speedily, into separations.

CHAPTER TWELVE

BRAND MARRIAGES AND THE
ENGAGEMENT IMPERATIVE

Emotions aren't mystical, wispy things that defy quantification. When it comes to brand relationships, the emotional connections that link people to brands have a definable structure. There is a foundation to this emotional structure — Confidence and Integrity. And there's a superstructure resting on this foundation — Pride and Passion.

These four components comprise the emotional brand bond. And the items developed to measure these four components provide a vital tool that companies can use to assess the health of their brand marriages.

But companies want and need to know the real value of an emotional bond. It certainly sounds nice to have one. It surely seems like a good idea to have a bevy of customers who feel passionate about the product or service we might be marketing. But how important is it — and what significance does it have for the financial bean counters and stock analysts? The question is, what kind of premium, if any, is an emotional connection really worth?

The answer: It's worth a lot.

BRAND MEASUREMENT FOR BRAND MANAGEMENT

Because companies need to establish the real value of their brand relationships, we developed and tested our customer engagement measures for their ability to provide companies with a rigorous, reliable quantitative indicator of what had previously required in-depth interviews, projective techniques, and focus groups. The result is a meaningful metric that can detect the key components that emotionally bond a customer to a brand.

This new engagement metric needed to:

1. *Provide a tool to enhance brand management.* We wanted to develop a useful outcome measure that companies could use to prioritize and guide the actions of company managers at all levels and all customer touchpoints. We wanted this measure to show a demonstrated relationship to things that managers can and should be able to influence, and thus, can and should be held accountable for. In short: It needed to provide *actionable* results.

   Note that there is a world of difference between "actionable" and "simple." "Actionable" does not mean that the necessary actions will be easy to implement. Nor does it imply that interventions can be begun immediately or by just involving the company's senior marketing leadership.

   Brand marriages may not be made in heaven, but they're also not made in the boardroom. Strong marriages require strong performance on all of the five Ps — performance that must be relentlessly and consistently applied and expressed at every meaningful customer touchpoint. That's where marriages are made — or destroyed. That's certainly not a simple challenge, but it's definitely actionable.

2. *Provide a measure that has clear and direct links to important business outcomes.* We wanted to establish a valid indicator for brand managers that reflects the health of their brand relationships and the real equity that's being built — or eroded — by their actions. We wanted a measure that would have credibility in the boardroom and even in the store. In short: The metric needed to be *meaningful.*

These engagement metrics needed substantial, demonstrable, and direct links to the business outcomes for which company managers are regularly held accountable. Otherwise, they would deserve no place in the balanced scorecard that guides resource allocation and serves as a focus for managerial action.

Making it actionable *and* meaningful — that was the challenge we faced in 2000 when we embarked on this excursion into the world of human emotions, brand marriages, and what we have termed "brand engagement."

BEYOND BRAND LOYALTY: BRAND ENGAGEMENT

To create an overall measure of "brand engagement," the set of eight brand attachment measures is combined with a commonly employed three-item measure of attitudinal loyalty. Gallup and others have used this three-item measure for many years as an index of a customer's intentions to continue his or her brand use or purchase and to advocate its use to others. The attitudinal loyalty measure consists of the following three rating scales that are combined into a single overall measure:

✦ Overall satisfaction

✦ Likelihood to continue/repurchase/repeat if needed

✦ Likelihood to recommend to others

This three-item measure provides for much greater stability than any single-item loyalty measure. Together, the three reliably indicate a customer's allegiance. By themselves, however, these loyalty items tend to reflect the rational, rather than the emotional, aspects of the customer relationship, including factors such as convenience and habit. Attitudinal loyalty is not a sensitive or revealing gauge of the important emotional connections between a brand and its buyers.

Thus, we've combined the traditional three-item loyalty measure with the eight-item brand attachment measure. The result is an 11-item metric of customer engagement called the CE^{11}. It's the ultimate measure of the strength and health of a brand marriage. (The full set of 11 ratings scales can be found in Appendix B.)

Together, the scales provide a complete assessment of the brand relationship, one that integrates both a customer's rational intentions along with his or her important emotional connections. They provide weight to both of these key decision-driving factors.

Based on their responses to these 11 items, customers can be meaningfully grouped into four distinct categories, as shown in the graphic "Customer Engagement Groups."

CUSTOMER ENGAGEMENT GROUPS

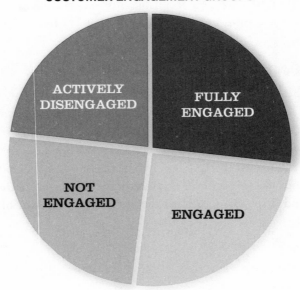

These four engagement groups were identified as a result of a number of business impact analyses that used the customer engagement measures to predict a number of relevant business outcomes. These outcomes included share-of-business, repeat business, level of business, volume of business, and profitability of business. As a result of these analyses, we identified four distinct levels of engagement. These describe four different types of customers, or customer relationships:

✦ *Fully Engaged*: These customers are both highly emotionally attached to the brand and strongly loyal. For every brand and category we've examined, they represent the highest value and best customers a company has. They spend more, return more often, are less price-sensitive, and stand tall as advocates and references. They are the happily and passionately married to the brand.

+ *Engaged*: These customers also have an emotional connection to the brand, though not quite as strong as that of the Fully Engaged customers. They are also somewhat less attitudinally loyal to the brand and less strongly cemented to continuing to buy or use it. They are certainly not dissatisfied, but for various reasons, they don't feel completely connected. They're married, but the relationship lacks the depth of passion and commitment of the Fully Engaged.

+ *Not Engaged*: These customers are essentially neutral to the brand; they feel a minimal emotional connection. In their eyes, the brand they are using is simply one of many. They may continue as brand users or shoppers, but that's a result of habit or expediency, not because they feel an emotional bond. These are the marriages of convenience.

+ *Actively Disengaged*: These customers have no connection to the brand. In cases where it's difficult for them to switch to another brand (for example, with their checking account or their mobile phone service) or where their options are greatly restricted (depending on their location, with airlines or with some retailers), they may be antagonistic — sometimes loudly so. In cases where switching is simpler, they may merely be disaffected and disinterested, with absolutely no allegiance to the brand. They are highly vulnerable, though they may see no real reason to switch if they view all brands as equally poor choices with equally poor performance. These are the customers who are most likely — and most eagerly — heading to divorce court.

We've found that these four groups are very different in their feelings about the brand and its representatives. They talk about the brand in very different ways. Importantly, they differ not just in their feelings and intentions, but in their *actions*.

THE SOUND OF ENGAGEMENT

Fully Engaged customers have a clear and discernible personal connection with the brands they're passionate about. These special brands no longer exist in a "sea of sameness." They've moved out of the realm of interchangeable alternatives into a new world where consumers talk about them as "their" brands — as an integral part of their lives. That's because they're convinced that there is something special about the brand, something delightfully different about how buying and using the brand makes them *feel*.

> "Minute Maid Orange Juice — that's how I start my day."

> "Home Depot. My husband and I need it. Don't ever take it away."

> "I don't think I would be able to live without CNN. I'm hooked on it."

> "Aveda encompasses everything that they stand for. They sell natural products. When you walk into the store, they have some sort of nice scent, and calming music going. The employees are really calm, and they're helpful. For me, it makes me feel stress-free when I'm in there. And I enjoy myself. It's very natural and soothing."

These voices can be heard in focus groups, large-scale surveys, and the books written by journalists reviewing the branded products and services whose stories they crave to tell. The following comments were made by David Kiley, a *USA Today* bureau chief, who writes about BMW in his recent book *Driven*:

> "Every time I slip behind the wheel, it leaps out at me — an authenticity and a sure-footedness ... Their design, performance under the hood, and the balance and agility of each vehicle are superb. Even when a competitor surfaces and achieves more horsepower ... most true car aficionados sense in their gut that those other cars are trying to be Bimmer beaters. [T]hese posers ... play a poor Jayne Mansfield to BMW's Marilyn Monroe."

The comments made by customers who really care about their brand are qualitatively different from the ways they talk about other brands. They may come in contact with or use other brands, but they feel no real emotional kinship with them. But these comments are not only qualitatively different; they're quantitatively different as well.

The size of these four engagement groups can vary considerably. Our research has identified brands where well over half of the current customers are Fully Engaged, but there are also brands with a dreadful shortage of happy marriages — where only 1 in 50 current customers are Fully Engaged.

THE WORLD OF CUSTOMER ENGAGEMENT

Fully Engaged customers, though they certainly aren't the norm, are also not as rare as might be expected. There are customers like this out there for almost every brand — even if, up till now, they've been largely undetectable. That's because they often don't choose to make themselves known, and most customer databases and satisfaction surveys can't separate the truly passionate from the merely habitual. Databases reflect customer behaviors, not their emotions.

A strong marriage is at its very foundation emotional, and the strength of a marriage cannot be measured by whether or not two people are currently living together.

Surveys have found that about 20% of a company's customers typically would qualify as being Fully Engaged. But that's only an average. That overall average masks huge and important variation — differences between categories (autos versus mobile phones), differences between brands (Honda versus Dodge) and — most surprisingly — differences between the stores, branches, call centers, sales groups, and dealerships that represent the very same brand.

It's perhaps most surprising that there is a great deal of variation within the same brand — in stores, for example, where the same layout displays the same products, which are being sold at the same prices.

In a study of one bank's customers, in some branches, more than a third (38%) of the customers were Fully Engaged. Yet in the same system, some branches, which were selling the same services under the same brand umbrella, didn't have a single Fully Engaged customer. Not one. Is this really one bank — or is it many very different banks?

In another study of a major retail chain, we found that its overall customer engagement levels were exceptionally strong, yet there was still a great range in store-level performance. Some stores had strong brand marriages with three-fourths of their customer bases. At the same time, other stores in that same chain had only one-third as many

Fully Engaged customers. The scores were strong, but there was still enormous variation in brand-building performance. Again, is this one store — or is it many?

We've seen this same pattern wherever there are multiple customer touchpoints. In branches and stores — and in fast-food outlets, distribution centers, and car dealerships — the data reveal that there is not one consistent level of customer engagement that exists across all company units. Rather, there are many different degrees of marriage-building performance. Some units are great at brand building, while others are terrible. Yet they have identical systems and are supposed to be equally capable in supporting the same brand promise.

CHAPTER THIRTEEN

THE VALUE OF A HEALTHY BRAND MARRIAGE

In recent years, we haven't just been digging into the measurement of customer engagement. We've also been investigating the impact of engagement — and the cost of customer disengagement.

Our deep dive has yielded a number of cases where customer engagement (CE[11]) metrics have been linked to key business outcomes. Some of these studies used a company's existing customer databases as the source for the business outcomes data. That's an advantage, because the data come not from customers' self-reported behaviors but directly from the hard-number databases from which the company's customers were sampled. Thus, the business outcomes in these cases are not subject to the self-reporting biases in which those who love something overstate their behavioral commitment.

Our research has addressed the question of business outcomes in two different ways. We conducted the first set of analyses at the individual customer level, directly contrasting the behaviors and spending of engaged and not engaged customers to compare healthy marriages with the not-so-healthy ones.

The second set of analyses examined unit-level business performance to determine the differences in customer engagement at the store, branch, dealership, or business-unit level. These unit-level analyses allow us to compare the business performance of stores with high versus low customer engagement and to look at the impact of changes in their engagement-building performance over time.

"SHOW ME THE MONEY" (PART I)

A study completed for a major bank in the United States shows the impact of customer engagement at the individual customer level. When we examined the overall level of engagement among checking-account customers, we found that just over 1 in 10 (11%) were Fully Engaged, while more than twice as many of their customers (28%) fell into the Actively Disengaged group. That's *not* a particularly encouraging picture. These engagement levels were the result of several company missteps, including some unsettled mergers that had left customers feeling unsettled. Yet there was still an important core of Fully Engaged customers, and their value quickly became obvious.

Analysis showed that the bank's Fully Engaged customers maintained total bank balances that were 26.2% greater than those of the Not Engaged or Actively Disengaged customers. They also maintained more accounts (almost 10% more). Quite literally, these customers were money in the bank. In the absence of a solid measure of emotional connectedness, these Fully Engaged customers had been largely invisible to the bank's management. But, whether or not the company recognized them, they were there — and they were quite valuable.

And missed opportunities among the company's disengaged customers were proving to be particularly costly. If this bank could have performed simply at the average for all banks noted in our U.S. banking-customer surveys, it would have doubled its number of Fully Engaged customers and increased its share of customer deposits. For this bank, the opportunity potential could yield additional total banking relationships worth just under $1.8 billion.

A second case involving a major grocery chain's customers provides additional evidence about the impact of customer engagement. Data from the grocer's database of membership club customers revealed that not all members of this group were equally loyal, committed, or enthusiastically bonded to the brand. The results also highlighted the important financial consequences that result from emotional connections.

Fully Engaged grocery shoppers, we found, visited the chain's stores more often. They went 8.9% more often than the Engaged customers — those who liked the chain, but didn't quite love it. And they visited an impressive 19.5% more often than the Actively Disengaged.

Why would a disengaged customer still shop there? The answer is simple: location, location, location. Bricks and mortar will buy some portion of a consumer's business, but never all of it — and it buys far less than if the customer were emotionally engaged. The Fully Engaged spent a lot more at the stores — almost a third (32.7%) more than the Actively Disengaged. And they gave the stores far more of their grocery-shopping business — about 80% of it, or about two-thirds more than the Actively Disengaged.

ENGAGEMENT PAYS. DISENGAGEMENT COSTS.

We've observed the positive economic consequences of healthy brand marriages in other companies and industries, too. Emotionally engaged cosmetics customers give their brand a share-of-purchase 77% greater than the share-of-purchase of those who are disengaged. Customers who are engaged with the brand of gasoline that they buy give that chain more of their business — 11.8% more — than do those who are not engaged. Emotion is a motivator in cosmetics, but it's also true even when it comes to buying a commodity like gasoline.

In other studies, we've found that customers who are engaged with a hotel chain give that chain a greater percentage of their hotel stays. For one large, well-known lodging chain, this amounted to a 64% greater share of nights spent at the hotel's properties for the Fully Engaged than for the Actively Disengaged. There are limits to the power of location and price. That's because when it comes to banks, grocery stores, gas stations, and hotels, consumers have options. And wherever there are options, the power of an emotional connection is powerfully evident and will have clear results.

What's more, the impact of customer engagement is just as powerful in business-to-business marketing. As stated earlier, business customers are also emotional — and those emotions, our studies have shown, have consequences. In the case of one cargo shipper, their engaged customers shipped 48% greater tonnage and spent 73% more money than their disengaged customers. Engaged physicians also reveal a similar pattern, giving a medical-products marketer an almost 50% greater share of their business than the disengaged doctors. Engaged financial-services brokerage customers accounted for a third (33.8%) more revenue than the disengaged, bought 50% more products and services, and also stayed with the provider longer (16.7% longer, on average).

Engagement pays off — and it pays off consistently.

Boosting engagement also pays off. In another banking study, Gallup examined the results of a series of initiatives and service improvements aimed at building Integrity and Pride. We found that customers whose engagement had increased also increased their total banking balances, which reflect their overall business relationship with the bank. Disengaged customers who moved, over the course of a year, into the Fully Engaged category increased their total deposits by 12%. Customers who were already Fully Engaged and maintained that high level also increased their total financial relationship with the bank by about 9%. Where engagement stayed low or slipped even further, so did the business relationship, declining on the order of 7%-8%.

Customer engagement pays off — and it *continues* to pay off. It serves as a bellwether of future financial performance. Engagement provides a clear signal, not just of the current state of a company's customer relationships, but of the economic consequences that will be felt for months and even years to come.

"SHOW ME THE MONEY" (PART II)

The payoff of customer engagement is also apparent at the unit level. There's plenty of ROI evidence for companies that regularly assess their performance, results, and profits at the store, branch, or dealer level, rather than at the per-customer level.

For one major home and do-it-yourself products retailer, researchers looked at the range of CE[11] scores, contrasting the top half of its stores with the bottom half, based on customer engagement. The researchers uncovered a difference of 7.6% in dollars per transaction. Stores that achieved higher levels of customer engagement achieved higher business volume for every transaction. Across the chain of stores, the engagement advantage added up to about half a billion dollars.

For another major retail chain, the results mirror what was found for the do-it-yourself retailer. Stores in the top half on customer engagement achieved higher sales per square foot — almost $20 more — than stores in the bottom half.

For an automaker, the business results were again impressive, revealing a familiar pattern. Looking at the performance of the top 25% of dealers based on their CE[11] scores, we noted that on every new vehicle they sold, they made 11.1% greater profit than the dealers that were in the bottom quartile. And by creating an environment where customers were pleased to return, they benefited in other ways: They also achieved significantly greater customer service income.

Customer engagement pays — and the stores that create higher levels of engagement show tangible evidence of the payoff. These stores have created environments where customers can *feel* the difference, and those warm customer feelings translate into cold, hard cash.

In addition, we've found that *increases* in store-level customer engagement also result in increases in sales and profit performance. For one large U.S. retailer, stores that increased their levels of customer engagement over the span of a year achieved sales growth that was more than 15% greater than that of stores whose engagement levels did not change — and 150% greater than that of stores where engagement levels declined.

Time and again, this pattern is apparent. The graphic "The Payoff of Customer Engagement" highlights just a few of the results we've observed. For any company, the conclusion is clear: *Engagement pays. Disengagement costs.*

THE PAYOFF OF CUSTOMER ENGAGEMENT

When Gallup compared Fully Engaged customers to Actively Disengaged and Not Engaged customers, we found that Fully Engaged customers:

BANK	maintained 26% higher bank balances
GROCERY CHAIN	shopped 20% more often and spent 33% more per month
COSMETICS MARKETER	had 77% greater share-of-purchases
GASOLINE RETAILER	had 12% greater share-of-visits
CREDIT CARD MARKETER	used 36% more frequently and spent 44% more per year

HOTEL CHAIN	had 64% greater share-of-business
CARGO SHIPPER	shipped 48% more volume and spent 73% more in total
BUSINESS SERVICES PROVIDER	yielded 34% greater revenue and 14% greater relationship longevity
DATA STORAGE PRODUCTS COMPANY	had 16% greater share-of-business
MEDICAL PRODUCTS MARKETER	had 50% greater share-of-business

When Gallup compared business units (such as stores, branches, or dealerships) with higher customer engagement to those within the same system but with lower customer engagement, we found that stores with higher customer engagement levels had:

HOME PRODUCTS RETAILER	8% higher dollars per transaction
AUTO MANUFACTURER	11% greater profit per new vehicle sold
BANK	$50,000-$200,000 higher quarterly profit per branch
MASS RETAILER	15% to 95% greater increases in same-store sales versus prior year
ANOTHER BANK	74% fewer loan defaulters
DO-IT-YOURSELF RETAILER	$20 greater sales per square foot

MORE MEANINGFUL METRICS FOR WALL STREET

It's no stretch to say that customer engagement provides a sharper and more relevant picture of brand health than do any number of other measures that companies and analysts typically rely on. Engagement reveals the extent to which a company has created strong — and valuable — brand marriages and it provides a sensitive monitor of the ebb and flow of the company's brand relationships.

That's not how most companies gauge their business success. In part, it's because they've had no credible metrics that could reliably reflect their relationship-building success. But it's also because that's not what Wall Street looks at. As a result, engagement hasn't been relied upon as one of the key factors that drive a company's stock value, even though it's abundantly clear that a company's *customers* ultimately determine the company's worth.

Wall Street, however, tends to value sales, market share, and volume growth. For an automaker, it's growth in the numbers of vehicles it sells and in the total profits it makes. For a soap maker, it's growth in market share and total profits. For retailers, it's total sales volume growth — but with special attention to same-store "comp" sales growth, or the volume increases seen in stores that have been open for at least a year.

Growth is the focus, even though research shows that bigger is not always better. Richard Miniter's *The Myth of Market Share* analyzes whether market share is an indicator of brand health, and concludes that it isn't. Miniter cites one study of 3,000 companies, which found that "more than 70% of the time, the firm with the biggest share of the market doesn't have the highest rate of return." The focus, Miniter contends — and we agree — should be on the customer, not on the competition.

That's a significant problem. Whatever a company identifies as a key goal will obviously become a critical objective that guides every company manager's plans and programs. For a good many of them, the goal will become an obsession and the cause of their sleepless nights.

So if the identified key goal is volume and share growth, managers will look to programs that will quickly and efficiently help to achieve them. Price-cutting is certainly one way; management can implement price reductions, deep discounts, and 0% financing. Products will move, at least in the short term, *but at what cost*?

If the key goal is company profits, then managers can pursue another direction, cutting the costs of doing business so these expenses can instead go directly to boost the bottom line. Profits will increase, at least in the short term, *but at what cost*?

Neither increased volume nor increased profits will necessarily benefit the real owner of the brand: the customer. And if there's no benefit to the customer, the company not only fails to enhance the brand marriage, it weakens it. When customer engagement slides, so do a great many other outcomes, including future sales, growth, and profit.

Instead, companies should focus on an objective that merits the diligent, even obsessive attention of the company's managers: customer engagement, and healthy brand marriages. Every manager should be laser-focused on building and protecting the company's most precious assets — its powerful and passionate customer relationships. These brand relationship assets determine the continued health and future success of the company.

CHAPTER FOURTEEN

≡BRAND MARRIAGE MANAGEMENT≡

Company CEOs and boards of directors are convinced that brands and customer relationships represent valuable assets. And they've shown a willingness to invest in these assets. Yet the evidence indicates that the effectiveness of company marketing programs and the returns on their brand-building expenditures are *not* increasing. Customer relationships aren't growing stronger. They're stagnant, mired somewhere in the realm of OK, woefully short of passionate.

Too many companies offer parity promises, parity performance, and a parity brand experience. Not surprisingly, prospects ignore their overtures, and their customers lack passion.

BEGIN AT THE BEGINNING

To address this problem, let's return to the beginning: the company's brand promise. The promise has an essential assignment. It must clearly establish the brand — and the feelings associated with being a brand customer — as meaningfully different from every other possible choice. Whether your brand is competing against 300 breakfast cereals, 3,500 IT consultants, or 30 midsize SUVs, the promise must establish a unique position in the minds of those who truly matter — the *consumers*. The brand must stand for something apart from the ordinary, something that merits consumers' attention and consideration, their business and, ultimately, their enduring allegiance and fidelity.

A brand differentiates itself most strongly and enduringly when it relates to how the experience of being a customer *feels*, whether that's driving a BMW down a back road, walking into a Wal-Mart store, taking a bite of a hot Taco Bell chalupa, or spreading Miracle Whip on a special club sandwich. Customers must feel the difference and be able to sense, recognize, and treasure it. If customers can't relate to anything, there's no basis for a personal connection.

Others have echoed this same sentiment. In *The Origin of Brands*, Al and Laura Ries argue forcefully that brands — and, we would add, brand *experiences* — must avoid the "mushy middle" where differentiation is minimal or unclear. In *Differentiate or Die*, Jack Trout warns of the "me-too" trap. He writes that blurred differences are the death knell of a brand, the reason why new brands flop and old brands wither away.

The lesson is never to get caught in the middle. As evidence, look to the struggles of companies like Kmart and Sears (which have now banded together), Ramada, Buick, A&P, and United Airlines; they're all stuck in the undefined middle.

Meaningful differentiation is fundamental — yet most brands can't pass this elemental test. Consumers can't identify what makes a given brand different from its competitors. There's no perceived difference from what other brands promise, and using or buying the brand doesn't give consumers a distinctive feeling. This holds true even for brands that customers have used for some time. When marketers ask a consumer, "What makes your brand different?" this is not the answer they want to hear: *"I don't know. I guess just the fact that I've used it for a long time."*

That is *not* a foundation for an enduring marriage. Consumers won't be confident that a company is determined and able to keep its brand promise if they have no idea what that promise *is*.

Too few brands are seen as different from their competitors. That's because woefully few companies have articulated what sets their brand apart from all others.

FOCUS, FOCUS, FOCUS

This lack of differentiation seems like an anomaly. After all, companies spend millions creating differentiated brand names, logos, and packages. They seem to know in their marketing bones that differentiation matters.

And companies do spend time wrestling with the differentiation challenge. "What do we stand for?" is quite likely to be the topic of a great many boardroom discussions. However, when it comes time for companies to state exactly what makes them different, then to carve that difference in corporate stone, they often shy away. Perhaps they just don't know what makes their brand experience different, or why that difference should merit a reciprocal relationship, let alone a brand marriage.

It's a common problem, yet it violates the fundamental requirement for business success that William Cohen laid out in *The Art of the Strategist*: "Commit fully to a definite objective." Unless the objective is clear and the company is fully and publicly committed to it, the chance of success is minimal.

In too many cases, though, the objective is murky, and the commitment isn't apparent. As Jim Collins points out in *Good to Great*, many companies have problems identifying what makes them different; very few know what they can promise, what they can provide, and what they can do better than anyone else in the world. Yet an emphasis on connecting with prospects and creating passion among customers requires that companies never settle for OK, and never pursue anything less than great.

Mediocrity in promise or performance does not build or maintain marriages. When it comes to brand marriages, there is no standing still. They get better, stronger, and healthier, or they deteriorate.

There's another problem related to the pursuit of "good enough." Most companies really want everyone to be a customer; they want everyone to marry them. Because of this, their brand experience is not crisply defined and sharply differentiated for a well-defined customer audience. They simply want their company to get really big, then get even bigger. That means more and more customers. They want their offerings to be universally appealing.

But there's no such thing — not if companies want real brand differentiation. No brand experience is equally appealing to everyone, and no brand should seek to do business with everyone. A brand that defines a category is either a monopoly or a generic. Either way, it won't become that special brand that will live and prosper within that category. And it won't sustain passionate brand marriages that are strong enough to withstand competitive overtures and the lure of lower prices.

No brand is a perfect fit for everyone.

IS BIGGER BETTER?

Nevertheless, corporate directors and Wall Street analysts still routinely embrace the mandate to grow, so growth has become the singular focus of most CEOs. That mandate drives marketers to continuously expand their vision of what they can and should promise, and to whom they should promise it. This leads to an ever-expanding brand promise and an ever-expanding, less-well-defined target audience.

It happens too often. *In Big Brands, Big Trouble,* Jack Trout points to General Motors as the poster child for the loss of focus that results from overextended brand promises. GM has offered increasingly larger, more expensive Chevys, along with smaller, less expensive Caddys, combining to squish the life out of poor, middle-of-the-road Oldsmobile.

GM isn't the only culprit. Volvo, having owned the world of safety, seeks to expand its world into the stylish and even sexy arenas. VW offers the Touareg SUV and the even more expensive Phaeton luxury sedan, while Porsche once toyed with a VW-powered mid-engine 914. We should probably be on the lookout for the launch of the compact Rolls convertible, the Jaguar minivan, and the nine-passenger Mini Cooper SUV.

In the automotive world, the mantra seems to be: First, define your differentiating brand promise, then expand that promise further into increasingly fuzzy territories. But that also sends this message to the current brand spouse, the Fully Engaged and committed brand loyalist: "We take you for granted. There's a much more exciting world beyond you, and that's where we really want to be." This doesn't enhance the clarity or the credibility of the company's brand promise.

Banks do this, too. They now sell everything from checking accounts and mortgage loans to insurance and investment advice. Telephone companies have expanded and merged from local to long distance and then, to everything from cable television to wireless

Internet communications. And the differentiated brand promise offered by this multi-service conglomerate is exactly — what?

No wonder consumers have a hard time defining what a given brand's promise actually is. Their confusion merely reflects the broad assortment of messages and products that issue forth from companies.

LIVING THE BRAND

An additional challenge emerges when companies can't articulate their brand promises, or when they stray from meaningful brand differentiation. Each company touches customers in a vast number of ways — through products, packages, and people; through promotions and publicity; through storefronts, parking lots, and employee uniforms; through Web sites and telemarketers. There must be consistency among all these touchpoints — all touchpoints must deliver one coherent brand message, and each touchpoint must fulfill the brand promise. If the message or performance is inconsistent, there will be inconsistency in how customers feel about their experience. And this will breed disengaged and dispassionate brand relationships.

Because of the complex ways in which companies come in contact with consumers, a well-articulated brand promise also has a vitally important *internal* purpose. A crystal-clear, differentiated brand promise will guide and focus the plans and activities at the company's consumer touchpoints.

Once the brand promise is developed, it absolutely must be *shared*. Product and design engineers, advertising departments, and store operations teams cannot hope to deliver and live the brand promise if they don't know what it is. Call-center teams, Web site designers, and store cashiers can't be expected to convey the same brand message — or deliver the same distinctive brand experience — when it's unclear or undefined.

One of the core measures of Gallup's 12-item employee engagement metric asks each person in the company the degree to which they can agree with this fundamental question: "I know what is expected of me at work." Without a clear definition of the company's brand promise, no one knows what's expected, and both employee and customer engagement suffer.

SOLUTIONS VERSUS SILOS

Another structural problem confronts companies that seek to enhance their connections with customers. Businesses have consumer contact in myriad ways — and consumers don't think of or treat them as distinct points of contact. Consumers see them as aspects of the same brand; they are components of the same overall brand experience. Each point of contact is a brand ambassador, an agent hired or commissioned on behalf of the brand.

Though consumers experience brands — whether it's Starbucks, Toyota, or Colgate — as integrated wholes, that's not necessarily how companies treat and manage them, and that's not how they structure their operations. Most companies divide their operations based on common activities or functions, not on how they're experienced by consumers. They create silos, each with a distinct functional responsibility: Marketing, Sales, Operations, Maintenance, Customer Relationship Management, Human Resources, Advertising, Legal, Quality Control, Production, Accounting — the list goes on.

On the surface, structuring into divisions facilitates the company's overall operations. It provides a common focus on one aspect of what the company does, and what it needs to do to stay in business. It concentrates business resources on identified needs.

Indeed, structuring into divisions makes a good deal of sense — unless you look at it from the customer's viewpoint. That's because the various functional areas aren't always in sync. Marketing may focus on expanding the company's marketplace and the appeal of its brand promise, while Legal focuses on reining in any hint of potentially culpable overpromise. Advertising focuses on creating messages to appeal to new customers, while the Customer Relationship department focuses on serving current ones and the Call Center focuses on shortening the average length of a phone call. All these groups have a direct impact on the quality of the customer experience, but only senior management has a purview that spans more than one or two silos. And a company's leadership is focused on the stock market, which means moving more volume and reducing costs.

THE BUCK STOPS WHERE?

All this takes place while the real owner of the brand relationship is walking into stores, waiting in line for an available teller, or trying to squeeze into seat 17B on the next flight to Denver. Or perhaps she's on hold, being told by a recording how important her phone call is, while being thanked for her patience — as though she had a choice.

So who is focusing on the customer? And we don't mean someone who shepherds a customer-complaints hotline or manages the e-mail offers sent to the customer database. We mean someone who's empowered to tap the full range of company resources to attract and retain passionately engaged customers.

In every company, certain functional areas have special emphasis, which recognizes the key roles they play in determining the organization's success. Companies have a CIO because technology management is increasingly critical, and every company needs a visionary champion with real clout. There's also a CFO, because finances are the firm's lifeblood. And there's a COO, serving as testimony to the key role of the company's total range of ongoing operations. There may even be a CMO (chief marketing officer), dedicated to coordinating advertising, promotions, packaging, and even pricing to grow the company's total business.

But where is the Chief Customer Officer? Where is the dedicated person who lives and dies for the customer, who wakes up every morning worrying about customer engagement? If the customer is really as important as the company's brochures and annual reports attest, there should be a person who holds sway over the full range of customer activities. It's probably not the CEO, because the needs of the customer and Wall Street aren't one and the same.

Appointing a Chief Customer Officer cannot represent simply a label change, where the title is slapped on whoever wrestles with customer complaints. The customer champion must have real clout — just like the CIO or CFO. Nothing that affects the customer should be undertaken without the CCO's direct and personal involvement.

Needless to say, creating and empowering such a "C-level" executive would be a huge challenge and a major step for most companies. But a few brave businesses, led by the innovative structures in place in some technology firms (e.g., Sun Microsystems and Cisco Systems), have established a Chief Customer Officer position, although the titles vary somewhat. If it's important for Sara Lee to have a CCO in its efforts to move more frozen cheesecake and essential for Kellogg's in its goal of selling more cereal, it should be every bit as significant for

Bank of America or Bristol-Myers Squibb or JetBlue. After all, isn't the customer as important as the laptops you purchase and the network you support?

Unfortunately, most current company structures don't facilitate a coordinated focus on designing, communicating, and delivering a delightfully distinctive brand experience. That's one reason why we've so often seen more than half of a company's customers being either completely indifferent (Not Engaged) or totally disconnected (Actively Disengaged). What a waste of potential! After crafting a compelling, differentiated promise capable of enticing prospects to try the product or service, the net result of the brand experience shouldn't leave half of its customers feel nothing or, worse yet, angry. And those customers will demonstrate their feelings with their angry voices as well as their wallets.

GETTING HEALTHY

But we're not irrevocably mired in a world in which half the customers are doomed to be disconnected, or where angry disaffection is more common than brand passion. It doesn't have to be that way, and some companies are proving it.

Companies are succeeding in creating customer engagement and they serve as best-practice examples of the power and potential of passionate brand relationships. One international business-services company we observed raised its brand Confidence scores by 46% over the course of a year. Changes like this have real meaning: A major U.S. retailer noted an increase of 1.1% in its market share for every increase of just 0.1 in its average overall CE[11] score. Increases in customer engagement aren't just fascinating to contemplate; they can actually happen. But that doesn't mean it's quick or easy.

And, though brand relationships can get better, it's clear that they won't unless there is real change, and companies take real action. Brand relationships won't grow stronger by just the act of measurement — whatever measure is used. And they won't get better just because another management memo tells everyone to pay attention to the customer.

They won't get better unless enhancing relationships becomes a genuine company priority, with clear objectives at every level, and at every point of meaningful customer contact. They won't improve if business proceeds as usual.

And they certainly won't grow stronger if companies focus on irrelevant or tangential outcomes. Brand awareness is not the goal. There are dinosaur brands in or near the bone yard that still boast high awareness. Advertising awareness is not the goal, either. If it were, Starbucks, the Mini Cooper, and Red Bull would be doomed; Oldsmobile would still be around; and Kmart would be a huge success.

The goal is and must be brand engagement — durably and measurably strong marriages between companies and their customers. This goal must be zealously and passionately pursued, not just in the boardroom, but also by everyone who stocks a shelf, answers a phone, redesigns a package, services a car, or creates a commercial.

There are best practices waiting to be shared. They've been waiting because, up until now, there was no reliable way to identify the pockets of relationship-enhancing excellence that might exist. Standard customer satisfaction surveys can't identify them, because they don't aim high enough. They ignore the real role of customer emotions, and they only rarely tie measurement to the individual touchpoints that make or break the bond between company and customer.

Best practices are lurking somewhere within every organization, and potential solutions are waiting to be implemented. First, they have to be identified. That means the range of possible actions — the "functional controllables" — must be examined to gauge their impact on the health of the brand marriage. Too many companies still look for the silver bullet, the magic solution that lends itself to immediate execution throughout the company: a new ad campaign, new cooking temperature requirements, a renewed focus on checkout speed, a redesigned ATM, new uniforms, smile buttons, an off-site pep rally.

But simple solutions simply don't work. What does work, we've found, are solutions that reach deep into the organization, drawing on the individual strengths of everyone who interacts with customers. The solutions that work clearly differentiate the brand experience or significantly and dramatically enhance the appeal and performance of the company's products or services. Companies need solutions that customers can feel, and that connect. But first, companies must recognize that when it comes to the brand experience, as former Nike and

Starbucks leader Scott Bedbury states in one of his brand principles: *"Everything matters."*

It's not easy, but what's the alternative? Sitting still, while more than half of your customers look for an opportunity to go elsewhere with some — or even all — of their business?

REQUIREMENTS FOR CONNECTING

We've sifted through more than 60 years of inquiry into consumer feelings, and we've gleaned some insights into what bonds consumers to the brands they've come to know, trust, and even love. The insights are clear, though they are far easier to state than to execute.

The longest journey begins with a single step, and the path to stronger brand marriages begins with these three points:

1. *Articulate your brand promise.* State exactly what you feel differentiates your branded product or service — not just rationally, but *emotionally*. To what extent do your prospects and customers agree that this makes you different? How widely known is your brand promise — both within the company and among prospects and customers? What are you doing to share that promise with those who need to know it? To what extent are you able to "own" that promise? What meaningfully compelling promise can you own, and how can you credibly support and convey it?

2. *Identify your target and state your goals.* Who are the consumers that you really want and need to engage? How is your customer base changing? Who are your most desirable prospects? What are you doing to identify and attract prospects who have the potential to form lasting brand marriages? What programs are in place to recognize and reward your existing customers? What are you doing to make certain you are emotionally connecting with and engaging your customers — not just satisfying them? Which customer needs — rational and emotional, overall and situation-specific — are you addressing in your efforts to create not just a differentiated promise, but a differentiated brand experience? How are you monitoring your progress and performance? How can you tell whether you're achieving your goals, reinforcing the health of your brand, and strengthening your brand relationships?

3. *Align your customer touchpoints.* In how many ways do you touch
   your prospects and customers — through your products, processes, people, policies, pricing, packaging, promotions, and
   places? How well is your brand promise known and lived at
   each of these touchpoints? How well are you delivering on
   your promise at each point of customer contact? How do you
   know? What kind of brand passion is evident among your
   people? What are you doing to ensure greater consistency, as
   well as performance excellence, at each customer encounter?
   Who is responsible and accountable for this? How well are you
   meeting the challenge to provide a single face to your customers and to your prospects? What obstacles stand in your way,
   and what is your plan for overcoming them?

Brand marriage management is not something to be undertaken
lightly or half-heartedly. Merely dipping the company's toe into the
engagement waters is not likely to yield results. William Cohen's first
principle is worth repeating: *"Commit fully to a definite objective."* A par-
tially funded pilot program will neither make the case nor meet the
challenge. Nor will the relationship-enhancement opportunity be ad-
equately addressed by another toothless, tangential task force or study
group that lacks passion or authority. Brand marriage management
requires alignment, immersion, and a depth of dedication that can be
felt throughout the organization. It's not for the timid, and it's certainly
not for the unprepared or uncommitted.

AND IN CONCLUSION ...

This book has told the stories of consumers — the people who
marry brands, and may even marry them for life. We've looked into
the world of brands through the eyes of the consumer, the company's
partner in a reciprocal relationship. The cases we've explored are
consumer-focused rather than company-focused.

After all, consumers make the choice to marry. Companies can
court. They can propose. They can hope to merit marriages, but they
can neither dictate dates nor require relationships.

Marriage counselors tell us that you have to work at a marriage,
and that's equally true for companies and brands. To work both harder
and smarter at this marriage management task, companies must look
to, and listen to, the consumer.

Stories about successful companies are important, and there are many of them. It's interesting to read about how GE "does it" or about 3M's approach to instilling a company-wide focus on innovation. It's fascinating to hear the stories of Nike and Nordstrom, of Disney and Intel. It can be educational as well.

But brand relationships can't be understood — nor can they be managed — without a thorough understanding of consumers' emotions and how and why they choose to get married. A company with no marriages is a company with no future.

Consumers are eager to tell you about the state of your brand marriages, and they're waiting to help you make those relationships better and stronger. It's vital to hear what they have to say — especially if you ask the right questions and are fully prepared to act on what you hear.

APPENDIX A

ENGAGEMENT POTENTIAL RATING SCALES

The set of scales listed below were developed to assess the potential for brand affinity, or a brand relationship, among a company's non-customer prospects. The ratings reflect prospects' feelings about the brand promise presented by a company through its various product, place, and people representatives and through its brand communications. The ratings are applied to a brand only if target consumers have at least some familiarity with the brand.

CREDIBILITY

✦ [Brand] is a name I can always trust.

✦ [Brand] always delivers on what they promise.

✦ [Brand] is a highly respected brand name.

✦ I know what [Brand] stands for and what makes them different.

COMPELLING

✦ [Brand] sets the standard for all other brands to follow.

✦ There is no other [product/service category] quite like [Brand].

✦ I can't imagine a world without [Brand].

✦ [Owners/Buyers/Shoppers/Customers] rave about how great [Brand] is.

CONNECTING

✦ [Brand] is the perfect [product/service category] for people like me.

✦ I can easily imagine myself as a [Brand] [owner/shopper/buyer/customer].

APPENDIX B

CUSTOMER ENGAGEMENT (CE¹¹) RATING SCALES

The set of 11 customer engagement rating scales that were used for the reported analyses are listed below. They provide a means to measure and monitor the strength of the relationship that exists between a company or a brand and its customers.

The metric consists of three attitudinal-loyalty rating scales, which use a 5-point scale that ranges from "extremely" (5) to "not at all" (1):

✦ Overall, how satisfied are you with [Brand]?

✦ How likely are you to continue to choose/repurchase/repeat (if needed) [Brand]?

✦ How likely are you to recommend [Brand] to a friend/associate?

These three attitudinal loyalty ratings are combined with a standard set of eight emotional attachment rating scales that also employ a 5-point scale, one that ranges from "strongly agree" (5) to "strongly disagree" (1):

✦ [Brand] is a name I can always trust.

✦ [Brand] always delivers on what they promise.

✦ [Brand] always treats me fairly.

✦ If a problem arises, I can always count on [Brand] to reach a fair and satisfactory resolution.

✦ I feel proud to be a [Brand] [customer/shopper/user/owner].

✦ [Brand] always treats me with respect.

✦ [Brand] is the perfect [company/product/brand/store] for people like me.

✦ I can't imagine a world without [Brand].

For product-marketing situations that don't involve a service component or human touchpoints, the two Integrity scales ("treats me fairly"; "If a problem arises, …") are adjusted as follows:

✦ [Brand] is a highly respected brand name.

✦ If a problem arises, I can always count on [Brand] to stand behind their products.

LEARN MORE

To keep up with the latest research and insights into customer engagement and brand management, visit the *Gallup Management Journal* at http://gmj.gallup.com, where William J. McEwen, Ph.D., and other marketing experts regularly contribute articles and case studies.

Readers of *Married to the Brand* can receive a complimentary 6-month trial subscription to the *Gallup Management Journal*. Simply go to https://commerce.gallup.com/ma/code/ and follow these instructions:

✦ If you already have a Gallup membership, enter your username and password, then click Log In.

✦ If you do not have a Gallup membership, click Create an Account and enter the required information. Click Submit Registration, then log in to continue. Enter your username and password, then click Log In.

✦ Enter the 6-month promotional code 512051247224747570, and click Continue.

✦ Review your order and click Submit Order if the information is correct.

For questions or assistance, e-mail galluphelp@gallup.com.

Are you married to a brand? To find out, take the online assessment in the *Married to the Brand* Book Center. You'll find this assessment, along with additional insights from the book's author, at the *Gallup Management Journal* Web site at http://gmj.gallup.com.

ACKNOWLEDGEMENTS

No book is ever a solo effort. It is the product of many labors and many minds. It derives from dedicated souls who contribute energy, urgency, and gray matter to the tasks of honing, shaping, and polishing — until, at some point, what was a rough and awkward structure begins to take on the form of a finished creation.

And so it is with this book.

The foundation for this endeavor rests directly on the legacy of an amazing visionary, Dr. George Gallup. More than 60 years ago, he established a tradition of asking the right questions, listening carefully, and scientifically sorting the answers, thereby giving meaningful voice to the previously unheard thoughts and feelings of millions of consumers. An important debt is also owed to David Ogilvy, whose early years at Gallup left an enduring mark on this company, fueled by his highly contagious passion for understanding brand relationships and building great brands.

The conceptual underpinning for this book is grounded in the past half-decade of midnight-oil discussions — and the considerable brainpower — provided by my fellow "godfathers of brand attachment": Bill Diggins and John Fleming. It could never have happened without them; they contributed enormously. Mere thanks don't express the depth of the debt.

The raw material (often painfully raw) was expertly buffed and groomed through the expertise of some remarkable editorial craftsmen, including the incomparable Geoff Brewer and the irreplaceable Barb Sanford, as well as tireless copyeditor Mark Stiemann and the exceptionally talented layout designer, Kim Goldberg. Thanks and appreciation go also to the panel of unnamed reviewers who provided thoughtful and helpful feedback on earlier drafts. The book was diligently shepherded by Piotr Juszkiewicz and hugely enhanced through the faith and creative energy of our own chief marketing officer and executive publisher, Larry Emond.

Yet there would have been nothing to polish or publish without the leaders around the Gallup globe who have continued to support the data-gathering and idea-sharing. Without them, there would have been plenty of opinions, but no solid science. People like great friend Andy Anderson, he of the unmatched intellect (and the great taste in merlot). Add to that CK Sharma, Kelly Aylward, George de Jager, Verapong Paditporn, Chris Stewart, Scott Ahlstrand, Rajesh Srinivasan, Jesus Rios, Nancy Marinelli, Eric Olesen, and Linda Slovic. Thanks also go to Alex Khoo, Tom Rieger, Xiaoguang Fang, Bob Tortora, Annette Templeton, Chris McCarty, Marco Nink, Michael Guo, Todd Johnson, Alec Gallup, Ping Zhang, Jeff Day, Johanna Godoy, Jen Krider, Anita Pugliese, Carole Hewitson, Hanhua Wang, Morris Wilburn, Gale Muller, Prasun Basu, Arthur Cesar, Ken Royal, Wendy McMullin, Rodd Wagner, Tao Wu, Raji Srinivasan, Jerry Hansen, Bing Liu, Dan Witters, Kevin Mu — and numerous project and interviewing teams that stretch from Shanghai to São Paulo and from Princeton to Prague. There would be no substance and precious few insights without their capable contributions. Importantly, this sharing process has been made possible through the leadership of Jim Clifton, who has created a climate at Gallup that not only encourages but requires digging deeper and reaching higher.

Acknowledgement must also go to those who've sculpted the rough clay of my own analytic capabilities and brand relationship management experiences. People like Brad Greenberg at MSU; Bill Wells, Keith Reinhard, and Marty Horn at Needham; Len Alaria and Jim Rice at D'Arcy; Bruce Mason and Dick Vaughn at FCB; Jerry Hanneman and Don Hempel at UConn; Clark Leavitt at Burnett; Ralph Watts at the

CMAB; Alec Biel at the Ogilvy Center; and Jack Tormey at McCann. These are the colleagues and mentors who've sharpened my focus over the years.

Included also are the clients whose brands and customers I've been fortunate to touch over the past three decades. Brands such as Nestlé, Gap Inc., Wells Fargo, Coors, Safeway, Intel, Cadillac, Wal-Mart, Sears, Lexus, Kraft, Green Giant, Disney, Helene Curtis, MCI, Hallmark, ARCO, SC Johnson, Sun-Maid, Chevron, IBM, Pizza Hut, Kleenex, Del Monte, and Bank of America. These brands have managed to merit their marriages.

And, harkening back to the essential legacies of both George Gallup and Don Clifton, gratitude and recognition must go to the thousands and thousands of consumers around the globe who've been willing and eager to talk to us about the brands with which they've bonded — and tell the tales of those that have fallen woefully short. The stories are all theirs.

But this sort of effort comes together and takes final form only through the ongoing encouragement (and patient understanding) of those who make it all seem worthwhile. And thus, most special thanks go to those who remind me daily of the power and value of a loving relationship. My wife and closest friend, Florence, to whom I dedicate this book. Also my family, Megan and James, Kathy, Kelsey and Patrick, my mom, Harriet, and my sister, Pat. For providing me with abundant and inescapable evidence of what it means to love, I owe them far more than this simple paragraph.

Married to the Brand